(Im)migrations, Relations, and Identities

Cynthia Dillard, *Series Editor*

Rochelle Brock and Richard Greggory Johnson III
Executive Editors

Vol. 54

The Black Studies and Critical Thinking series
is part of the Peter Lang Education list.
Every volume is peer reviewed and meets
the highest quality standards for content and production.

PETER LANG
New York • Washington, D.C./Baltimore • Bern
Frankfurt • Berlin • Brussels • Vienna • Oxford

Chinwe L. Ezueh Okpalaoka

(Im)migrations, Relations, and Identities

Negotiating Cultural Memory, Diaspora, and African (American) Identities

PETER LANG
New York • Washington, D.C./Baltimore • Bern
Frankfurt • Berlin • Brussels • Vienna • Oxford

Library of Congress Cataloging-in-Publication Data
Okpalaoka, Chinwe L.
(Im)migrations, relations, and identities: negotiating cultural memory,
diaspora, and African (American) identities / Chinwe L. Ezueh Okpalaoka.
pages cm. — (Black studies and critical thinking; vol. 54)
Includes bibliographical references.
1. African diaspora. 2. Africans—Migration.
3. Group identity. I. Title.
DT16.5.O396   305.896'073—dc23   2013026129
ISBN 978-1-4331-2226-2 (hardcover)
ISBN 978-1-4331-2225-5 (paperback)
ISBN 978-1-4539-1203-4 (e-book)
ISSN 1947-5985

Bibliographic information published by **Die Deutsche Nationalbibliothek**.
Die Deutsche Nationalbibliothek lists this publication in the "Deutsche
Nationalbibliografie"; detailed bibliographic data is available
on the Internet at http://dnb.d-nb.de/.

Cover photo by Chineze Okpalaoka

© 2014 Peter Lang Publishing, Inc., New York
29 Broadway, 18th floor, New York, NY 10006
www.peterlang.com

All rights reserved.
Reprint or reproduction, even partially, in all forms such as microfilm,
xerography, microfiche, microcard, and offset strictly prohibited.

This book is dedicated to my children: Ugonna, Chineze, Dubem and Amara. May the wisdom of your foremothers and forefathers shine through these pages. You, too, are bridges across the waters. May you always remember the place we call home through the voices of all the African immigrants who find themselves in voluntary and involuntary exile in the diaspora.

Contents

Series Editor's Foreword ix
Acknowledgments xiii

Chapter 1-**(Im)migrations, Relations, and Identities of African Peoples**:
Toward an Endarkened Transnational Feminist Praxis
in Education (with Cynthia Dillard) 1

Chapter 2-**On Naming**:
Contestations and Nuanced Complexities
in Naming the Feminist Spirit 27

Chapter 3-**The Diploma Belongs to Us**:
Mentoring African Immigrant Girls Through/
For the Community 51

Chapter 4-**Wisdom Lost and Regained**:
My Life as a Generational Bridge
Across Three Migrations 67

Chapter 5-**Cultural Memory as Endarkened Feminist Methodology**:
Maintaining National Voice in the African Diaspora
Through (Re)membering 83

Chapter 6-**"What's in a Name?"**
The Names We Bear and (Im)migrant Ethnic
Identity Development 101

Epilogue-**"What Nation You Is?"**
Negotiating Diaspora and African Identities—
Which Way Forward? 119

References 123

Series Editor's Foreword

To write of (im)migrations and Black identities is to put into words the memories of the ancestors. It is to bless our mothers and fathers "whose migration made [us] possible, and to the millions of others like them who dared to act upon their dreams" (Wilkerson, 2010, p. v). It is to weave the geographical, political, social, and historical truths of our lives as African people—fragmented and whole, attached and displaced (maybe all at the same time)—into strips of regal kente that represent the cultural memories we produce everyday, everywhere…bell hooks (2009) says:

> We are born and have our being in a place of memory. We chart our lives by everything we remember from the mundane moment to the majestic. We know ourselves through the art and act of remembering. Memories offer us a world where there is not death, where we are sustained by rituals of regard and recollection…[here], I pay tribute to the past as a resource that can serve as a foundation for us to revision and renew our commitment to the present, to making a world where all people can live fully and well, where everyone can *belong*. (p. 5, emphasis mine)

To write of migration then is to write of the emotional truths that we have lived as Black women, to engage in a re-telling of what goes on inside of us, our spiritual lives, our collective and individual motivations, the truths we live when the masks we too often wear are set aside. Embracing an ethic that opens to spirit is fundamental to the nature of learning, teaching, and by extension, research. We recognize that such spaces and acts—and our memories and ways of being with/in them—are always and in all ways also political, cultural, situated, embodied, and spiritual. They are *alive* and present within us. However, all too often, we have been seduced into forgetting (or have chosen to do so), given the weight and power of our memories and the often radical act of (re)membering in our present lives and work. But to write of the truths of our (im)migrations, movements, and spiritual locations, we must learn to (re)member the things that we've learned to forget. We must learn to (re)member these movements and (im)migrations and in order to answer several questions of our lives: **What does it mean to belong? Do I want to belong? What are the real consequences of not belonging?** One answer many African ascendant people already know is that often our (im)migrations have been acts of dispossession from our memories of the past, from connections to our culture, original homelands, languages and from one another. But one thing I know? These memories *matter*. They are the spiritual and sacred (re)search that African people have always done and continue to do, given persistent and long standing oppressions, exclusions, and misrepresentations within both educational settings and the broader societies within which we live.

So to write of the impacts and influences of (im)migrations on our identities is to write of deliberate acts of piece making. Acts of gathering and assembling fragments of our identities here, there and everywhere. Acts of being, creating and producing new locations that are always already between and amongst. These are also acts of consciousness-making: Of choosing to write our identities out loud instead of choking silently on them. Mostly, as we write these identities, we write not just stories of belonging but of *becoming*. Of becoming (and being positioned) "Black." American. Nigerian. Feminist. Womanist. Been-to. "Intelligent and articulate." Crafting and creating these stories is to recognize the need for both new names and old names, new definitions and old ones to be able to walk over sometimes treacherous chasms on unstable rope bridges—and to keep on steppin'.

(Im)migrations, Relations, and Identities: Negotiating Cultural Memory, Diaspora, and African(American) Identities by Chinwe L. Ezueh Okpalaoka holds our hand on that very journey, providing an in-depth look at the role that cultural memory, history, time, displacement, and geographical location have played in African (im)migrations and the dynamic nature of Black identities marshaled within and across national contexts. In her walk and in these pages, Chinwe Okpalaoka provides powerful insight into the ever changing meanings of becoming and belonging for West African immigrants, inner sights that enlarge our understanding of taken for granted meanings of migration, immigration, identity, culture and nation. Through careful research that is biographical, ethnographical and case-studied in nature, she illuminates important dimensions of the (im)migrant experience, those unsteady socializations, and nuanced cultural memories that are important in the education of Black children. She also helps us to see that education for our children extends far beyond the school, encompassing the socio/cultural values and spiritual traditions of Black people. In these pages, she deftly marshals illuminating stories rich with African referents like hair braiding, generational story-

telling as bridges, accents and voice, the power of our names and naming. *(Im)migrations, Relations, and Identities: Negotiating Cultural Memory, Diaspora, and African (American) Identities* helps us to answer two very powerful questions facing society and education today. First, how do we develop a new understanding of the terms African and American by placing them in a global context (and even putting the "American" in parentheses to designate those born of African people brought to the United States during the transatlantic slave trade)? Considering that the demographics of American schools continue to reflect the rapidly changing faces of (im)migrants (including increased Black African immigrants), this book troubles the very notion of the names we call ourselves as a way towards productive dialogues and discourses about who Black people are and how we might belong and become *together*. The second central question of this book: How do we acknowledge the roles of both time and terms of "arrival" in current definitions and namings of who is African (American)—and how? Okpalaoka cogently explores this tension that exists in both our schools and our societies and argues that it is partly bound up in the ways that identity for Blacks in America is shaped by the timing and the mode of arrival to the United States between more contemporary African immigrants and African people born in the United States, most often as a result of the transatlantic slave trade. Chinwe Okpalaoka approaches these very complicated questions with a kind of (un)certainty that is a provocative echo and an illustrative embodiment of the very dynamism of Black identity she puts forth in this book.

As the Series Editor for the *Black Studies and Critical Thinking—Spirituality and Indigenous Thought* sub-series, I have been blessed to watch the years of development of this very beautiful and powerful look at (im)migration and Black identity. At times I was an intimate participant, sharing ideas and experiences as we worked together to better understand the influences and spirit of movement, time, and space for African people. Other times, I stood more at arm's length, which allowed me to see the elegance in Dr. Okpalaoka's story weavings. Hers is an enactment and engagement with sometimes painful stories and memories that I believe leaves the reader heartbroken and healed at the same time. For me, as a Black feminist scholar, *(Im)migrations, Relations, and Identities: Negotiating Cultural Memory, Diaspora, and Afri-*

can(American) Identities represents a kind of global feminism in the best sense of the words. This is an important gift of wisdom and legacy from Black women of the world, given to those who choose to *become* even more of themselves through reading it.

Cynthia B. Dillard, Ph.D.
(Nana Mansa II of Mpeasem, Ghana, West Africa)
Mary Frances Early Professor of Teacher Education,
The University of Georgia

References

hooks, b. (2009). *Belonging: A culture of place.* New York: Routledge.

Wilkerson, I. (2011). *The warmth of other suns: The epic story of America's great migration.* New York: Vintage.

Acknowledgments

No author arrives at the conclusion of their work without the support of others. The writing of this book could not have been possible without the support of family, friends and colleagues. This work is a culmination of a series of small steps on a long journey in the art of writing

First, I thank God who continues to order my footsteps daily. There truly is a time for every purpose on the earth. There has been a time of incubation and now is the time of birth;

To my family: I thank my husband, Osita Okpalaoka, for partnering with me as we walk out our life purposes together. Your love and patience are precious. And to our children, Ugonna, Chineze, Dubem and Amara for the joy you bring to my life. Your amazing humor has brought much laughter and joy to my life;

To my father and mother, Micah and Cecilia Ezueh: I am happy that you are here to witness the birth of my first book. You sowed the seeds of learning and excellence very early in your children and pushed us to excel academically;

To my siblings, Ngozi, Nkem and Ik: Although distance and time have separated us, I am thankful that when we do reconnect, the memories we share make it seem like we were never apart;

To Dr. Cynthia B. Dillard: Thank you for assuming the roles that you have in my life. I am honored to call you sister scholar, friend, mentor, teacher, and now Series Editor of the Spirituality and Indigenous Thought series. Your faith in me has stretched me in an unimaginable way;

To Chris Myers, Managing Director at Peter Lang Publishing, and Rochelle Brock, for your support as we push forward the conversation around spirituality and indigenous thought;

To Sophie Appel, Design and Production Supervisor at Peter Lang Publishing, for your grace and patience with my numerous calls for help with the formatting of this book.

PHOTO ACKNOWLEDGMENT: Betty's Bay, Western Cape, South Africa from the personal collections of Chineze Okpalaoka.

PERMISSIONS: Chapter 1 (co-authored with Cynthia Dillard) is a slightly revised version of Okpalaoka,C.L. & Dillard, C.B. (2012). (Im)migrations, Relations and Identities of African Peoples: Toward an Endarkened Transnational Feminist Praxis in Education. *Journal of Educational Foundations*, 26(1-2), 121-142.

Chapter 1

(Im)migrations, Relations, and Identities of African Peoples

Toward an Endarkened Transnational Feminist Praxis in Education

WITH CYNTHIA DILLARD

I'll see some Black people, I'll think they are Africans and they can understand you, but they're really prejudiced and racists, like [when you] come from Nigeria, they'll be like, "Oh, you're African!" [in a derogatory tone] and I'll say, "What are you? You are African, because your ancestors are." But I don't think they understand the reason, like they don't appreciate their culture and they're really prejudiced against us." (Ekene, personal interview, March 2008)

Because that's just the way they are.... They always go and be prejudiced. Even at this school, they look at you "Oh, you are African," and I say, "Yeah so are you." (Ekene, personal interview, March 2008)

Thank you so much for letting me take part in your study. It has made me begin to ask myself, "Who am I? An African American or Ghanaian?" But like I told you sometimes I consider myself a Ghanaian, because I am happy to have a background, to actually be from somewhere.... (Abena, participant journal entry, March 2008)

Who is an African? Which group of people can rightly lay claim to an African identity? Is an African identity the sole right of a particular group of people? These are questions that are being asked in the corridors of our homes, schools, and even our government, with the growing migrations of contemporary Africans and the election of the first African American president of the United States of America. In schools where the presence of contemporary African immigrant children is noticeable, these questions are being asked in various formats in interactions with their African American peers. Even in multidisciplinary conversations about African identities, scholars have been preoccupied with approaches to this question that span the fields of anthropology, literature, history, and political science (Yewah, 2008). On the African continent itself, with its diversity of language, politics, religion, and history, these questions have also been illustrated by a volume edited by Adibe (2009). In this book, scholars such as Ali Mazrui, Kwesi Prah, Gamal Nkrumah, Helmi Sharawy, and Marcel Kitissou tackle the perennial question of what it means for Africans on the continent and in the diaspora to be linked with an identity that is laden with much history, connotations, and misunderstandings. Speaking of an African identity that is not static, Achebe (1992) has this to say:

> It is true that the African identity is still in the making. There isn't a final identity that is African. But, at the same time, there is an identity coming into existence. And it has a certain context and a certain meaning. Because if somebody meets me, say, in a shop in Cambridge [England], he says, "Are you from Africa?" Which means that Africa means something to some people. (quoted in Appiah, 1992, p. 73)

Whether we consider the earlier involuntary or recent voluntary migrations of Africans to the United States, conversations about an African identity are timely when we consider that the descendants from both "migrations" are now learning side by side and interacting in ways that are pushing backroom conversations about African identities to the forefront. African immigrant children and their African American peers are engaged in critical conversations about their perceptions of what an African identity might look like. Undergirding these perceptions are dominant discourses about Africans and African Americans (Okpalaoka, 2009a; Okpalaoka, 2009b; Traore, 2006).

As seen in the quotes that begin this chapter (Okpalaoka, 2009a), in order to answer the question of who we are as African ascendant people, we need to take a closer look at the role that history, time, displacement, and geographical location have played in our migrations and the dynamism to the nature of the identities we adopt within and across national contexts. The notion of ascendancy, as it relates to African people, is attributed to Kohain Hahlevi, a Hebrew Israelite rabbi, who coined the term African "ascendant" as opposed to African "descendant" to describe people of African heritage and their forward-moving nature. According to him, the term "descendant" may imply a downward or backward-moving process. In the same vein, ascendancy implies a progressive movement that calls on us to consider a different language or discourse for the ways we talk about people of African origin.

(Im)migrations, Relations, and Identities of African Peoples

Looking within ourselves and our common history to (re)member who we are is critical to confronting dominant discourses that seek to define us. But remembering who we are means that we have to address the dearth of knowledge about Africa, Africans, and the African (im)migration experience in our society and in our schools. While research and the literature have kept pace with the experiences of major immigrant groups such as Asians (Zhou, 1999; Takaki, 1998), Latino/as (Suárez-Orozco & Todorova, 2003; Suárez-Orozco & Suárez-Orozco, 1995), and Black Caribbeans (Waters, 1991, 1994), there is still a noticeable dearth of research about Black African immigrant children (Rong & Preissle, 1998). Rong and Brown (2002a) argued that "the lack of research on Black immigrants denies the American public and policy makers opportunities to explore the many urgent and intriguing issues concerning Black immigrants, therefore denying the public insight into the special needs of these immigrants which have been neglected" (p. 249).

The focus of this chapter will be on examining the sense of what an *African* (American)[1] identity could mean when viewed through the processes of migrations and fluid identities of contemporary African immigrant children as they interact with their African (American) peers in our schools. The purpose of this chapter is to use data[2] from a study of West African immigrant girls and their process of ethnic identity construction to support our position for new discourses and methodologies that challenge the dominant discourses surrounding the Black educational experience in our schools. This purpose can be articulated in two central questions that guide this chapter. First, how do we develop a new understanding of the variations of the terms African and American by placing them in a global context (and the "American" in parentheses to designate those who were born of African people brought to the United States during the transatlantic slave trade)? Considering that the demographics of American schools continue to reflect the changing faces of immigration due to the increase in Black African immigration, this chapter will trouble our rather taken-for-granted notions of the term/name African (American).

Second, how do we acknowledge the role of temporality in current definitions of who is African (American)? The tensions that exist, represented in the voices that began this chapter, cannot be separated from the timing and mode of arrival of more contemporary African immigrants and African (Americans) in the United States and how claims are made to the label African (American). The goal of this chapter is to examine the issue of appropriate naming of African ascendant people in the United States and to examine how asking new questions about who we are might lead to a more global framework for studying identity construction and negotiation for African ascendant people in the United States. When we understand the way identity is being marshaled and used by African ascendant schoolchildren and the ways in which they are negotiating their identities similar to or different from existing discourses, we will begin to ask new and/or different questions of them and ourselves. Educators will be able to reconsider how classroom and school discourse might better reflect the ways that varying notions of African (American) identity impact the school experiences of the Black student. But this can only occur within a context that places African ascendant people's experiences and movement in(to) the United States historically. The following section both explores and troubles the notion of identity and migrations of African ascendant people in a way that seeks to better understand the fluidity of Black identities in the historical and geographical contexts that we have occupied and continue to occupy. We start by explaining some of the dominant discourses that have sought to name the reality of who we are, as African ascendant people.

Troubling Dominant Discourses about African and Black Education

Much of the dominant discourse that has framed conversations about African (Americans) and education in the literature has been couched in a narrative of inferiority, pathology, and underachievement. These discourses not only frame the rank and status that African (Americans) have or do not have in society or the ways that African (Americans) are perceived in society, but they particularly shape the ways that African (Americans) are represented as problematic in educational research. There has been a "preponderance of deficit-model...research that pathologize[s] African American youth and reproduce[s] notions of African American intellectual and social inefficacy" (Brown, 2005, p. 63). The origin of deficiency discourse in education dates back to the period from the early 1960s to the 1970s when social agencies, including schools, began to engage in the pathologizing of African (American) children. School desegregation was in full swing at that time, and the influx of Black children into previously all-White schools led to the emergence of labels that portrayed Black children as "culturally deprived"/"culturally disadvantaged" (Reismann, 1962), and, much later, "at risk" (U.S. Department of Education, 1998). Although some of these terms have been discontinued in the research lexicon, the discourse that still dominates is one that portrays Black children as always already less successful than their White counterparts. Most often, this "underperformance" is largely linked to their race and class.

Other discourses that have entered the conversation on the education of Black students have been based on racial identity theories and the implications for Black students' education. Helms's (1990) definition of racial identity emphasized the social and political implications of group membership and the subsequent effect on individual psychological functioning. As the most widely studied constructs among African (Americans), Helms's (1990) and Cross's (1995) racial identity theories explained the process by which individuals develop attitudes and beliefs about racial group membership. According to Helms (1990), racial identity theory refers to "a sense of group or collective identity based on one's perception that he or she shares a common heritage with a particular racial group...[and] racial identity theory concerns the psychological implications of racial-group membership, that is, belief systems that evolve in reaction to perceived differential group membership" (p. 3). In a society where racial group membership is emphasized, the development of a racial identity is inevitable in some form for everyone (Tatum, 1997). These notions of Black identity formation resulted in studies that illustrated a variation in the way that not only Black students, but also ethnic minority students, self-identified, and the subsequent effect of their ethnic identity on their schooling process (Ogbu, 1987; Fordham, 1996; Waters, 1991, 1994; Rong & Brown, 2001). These studies were supported by Fuligni, Witkow, and Garcia (2005), who contended that when it comes to schooling in the United States, ethnic minority groups are stereotyped according to their attitudes toward schooling and their academic performance. Scholars such as Fordham and Ogbu (1986) became well known for ascribing oppositional identities to Black students from different socioeconomic backgrounds when they failed to perform well academically so that they would not be perceived as "acting white."

Since Fordham and Ogbu's (1986) work, other studies have challenged the association of ethnic identity strength and academic achievement. Phinney (1992) argued that students with more developed levels of ethnic identity performed better in schools than those with less developed ethnic identity. Sandoval, Gutkin, and Naumann (1997) found a close relationship between African (American) adolescents' academic achievement and racial identity attitudes. Fuligni and colleagues (2005), in their study on the implications of ethnic identity on adolescents' academic motivation and achievement, concluded that the strength of their ethnic identification was relevant to their academic adjustment. Despite the mixed opinions of researchers on the influence of ethnic/racial identity development on school experience, researchers such as Banks (1993) and Rong and Brown (2001) are among those who support enhancing adolescents' ethnic identity development for better academic achievement and general school experience.

In addition, there are other discourses that specifically (and negatively) characterize the Black female as the matriarch (overly aggressive and unwomanly), the mammy (obedient servant), and the welfare recipient (lazy, poor, and dependent on welfare state entitlements) (Collins, 2000). All of these labels have been used to justify not only Black women's oppression, but also the oppression of African (Americans) as a whole (Collins, 2000). Since schools, among other agencies, are complicit in reproducing these discourses, these stereotypes are likely to be played out in the school interactions between African (American) students and their peers.

Whereas most of the dominant discourses discussed above have originated from European hegemonic views of African (Americans) in the United States, many of them have also been adopted within the African diaspora and on the continent of Africa and have shaped the pre-migratory perceptions that many immigrant groups have of African (Americans). Some of these discourses center on stereotypes of African (Americans) held by Africans on the continent who, though they may never migrate to the United States, have been influenced by media depictions of African (Americans) as violent and lazy. Those who do migrate to the United States then bring these notions of African (Americans) with them, which may culminate in tense relations in the schools and society (Traore, 2006; Okpalaoka, 2009a).

In addition to the stereotypes of African (Americans) that African immigrants bring with them to the United States are the stereotypes of Africans held by African (Americans) in the United States. The dominant discourse around African immigrants is that they are hungry, poor, diseased, and uncivilized (Traore, 2006; Okpalaoka, 2009a). Findings from Okpalaoka's (2009a) study indicate the recurrence of statements such as:

> *Eww, she's from Africa. She needs to go back where she came from....You have weird hair. You smell weird. You do stuff weird.* (Ekene, personal interview, March 2008)

> *Yeah, 'cause usually what they be seeing on TV, they think that Africans just look dirty, nasty and poor....Well, when they found out [that my parents were from Nigeria], they said, "Do you see lions and tigers running across your bedroom when you're there?"* (Amanda, personal interview, March 2008)

The tension that arises between both groups speaks to a historical and cultural disconnect and a seeming lack of kinship between African immigrants and African (Americans) in the United States. The disconnect often leads to the former embracing a strong African identity in resistance to the stereotypes they face or to their own stereotypes of African (Americans) (Okpalaoka, 2009a). African (Americans), on the other hand, may distance themselves from the negative stereotypes that they have been taught and hold about Africans or may feel that they have lost (or never had) a connection to the continent and its people through the disruption caused by the transatlantic slave trade.

The United States has been witnessing a period in its history referred to as the fourth wave of immigration, which has led to what Rong and Brown (2002b) have called the "largest racial/ethnic transformation in history" (p. 123). Among the groups that have been significantly represented in this immigration wave are Black immigrants from Africa and the Caribbean (Rong & Brown, 2002b). According to the U.S. census, about 2 million West Indians were living in the United States in 2002. Between 1965 and 1992, it is estimated that over 2.25 million people migrated from Africa to the United States (Kamya, 1997). Forty-seven percent of African immigrants are Black, with a third of this population coming from Nigeria (Djamba, 1999). Therefore, Nigeria is believed to be the largest sender of West African immigrants, followed by Ghana. This explains the national backgrounds of the participants in Okpalaoka's (2009a) study from which the data used in this chapter were obtained.

Population projections by Edmonston and Passel (1992) placed the number of Black immigrants and their children at about 12% of the U.S. Black population by 2010. Nowhere else is this demographic transformation reflected more than in our schools. Olson (2000) argues that our schools are now confronted with educating the most racially and ethnically diverse student body in our nation's history. This includes *within and between* Black ethnic groups. How do these changing demographics affect the ways we talk about the *Black* child and education? And how do the changing demographics of Black America impact the discourse about African *and* American identity, considering that "the problem is that many Americans hold a monolithic view of the Black community" (Rong & Brown, 2002a, p. 252)?

Questions in educational research so far have determined the answers we have constructed about Black children in our schools. But with the movement of African ascendant people in the world today, we must also consider the variations inherent in the label African (American) and ask new questions. Might we use more global frameworks to do research with and for African ascendant people, with the understanding that both identity positions, African and African (American), are legitimate spaces from which we can do this work? Could there be simultaneity, from the local to the global, in educators' approach to classroom and school discourse when we talk about the Black student? One of the ways to extend the meaning of these identity constructions and to develop more appropriate frameworks for the work we do for and about African ascendant people in all our variations is to begin with an understanding of the variations in our (im)migration experiences and histories.

Unpacking (Im)migration:
Troubling Black Identities Through Time

> *I'm proud of my heritage because most [African (American)] people, they don't know where they're from....I'm from somewhere.* (Ekene, personal interview, March 2008)

In response to the negative stereotypes about her African heritage that she encountered in school, the above statement was made by a first-generation African immigrant girl to distinguish her immediate traceable roots to Africa from her African (American) peers, whom she perceives as not being able to lay claim to similar roots (Okpalaoka, 2009a). The idea that only contemporary African immigrants "know where they're from" necessitates our troubling of the notion of what it means to be Black in our schools and what an understanding of the inherent variations in that label might mean for educators. A brief look at the origin of African (Americans) in the United States is important as we attempt to situate African immigrant and African (American) experiences with identity within the discussions surrounding dominant discourses in education.

The transatlantic slave trade, which began in the fifteenth century, saw the largest forced migration in history, resulting in the substantial presence of African people on North American shores (Arthur, 2000). When legal enslavement in the United States ended with the passage of the Thirteenth Amendment in 1865, immigration of Africans born on the continent of Africa was at a bare minimum. It was not until the first 50 years of the twentieth century that African immigration picked up as a result of colonial rule in Africa (Gordon, 1998). The number of Africans who have settled in the United States in the past 25 years represents the largest number of Africans to have settled here in more than 200 years (Arthur, 2000). Their presence in major cities of the United States such as Houston, Los Angeles, New York, Washington, D.C., and Atlanta cannot be ignored. And the presence of their children in our schools, learning alongside and interacting with their African (American) peers, has raised questions about the meaning of "African" identity and the sociocultural context of teaching and learning. Below we provide a brief history of the process of (im)migration to the United States of African ascendant people, both historically and contemporarily. We attempt to show how two groups of people from the same continent, having arrived in the United States at different times in history and through markedly different means, have created a particular relationship within and between African people. We suggest that an understanding of these dynamics might push us to consider a framework for educational research with/in these populations that can "talk back" (hooks, 1989) to dominant discourses, one that is endarkened (Dillard, 2000) and embraces notions of both transnationalism and feminism (Dillard & Okpalaoka, 2011) in education and research with/in this increasingly diverse school population.

Background: History of African (American) Migration

African presence in the United States dates back to the early 1600s, when it is recorded that a Dutch ship in Jamestown, Virginia, exchanged its cargo of 20 Africans for food (Bennett, 1984). Therefore, the history of the arrival of African (Americans) to the United States must begin with this group that Berlin (2003) calls the "charter generation...cosmopolitan men and women of African [ascent] who arrived in mainland North America almost simultaneously with the first European adventurers" (p. 6). Although the charter generation was an indentured group, they enjoyed a freedom of movement and material acquisition in what was "a society with slaves" as opposed to "the slave society" of later generations (Berlin, 2003, p. 55).

By the late 1600s, a switch from indentured White labor to African slave labor occurred as the "plantation generation" (Berlin, 2003) began to arrive in slave ships. Unlike the first group, which had hopes of eventual freedom, these groups were torn from their homelands and brought to the United States to satisfy the labor and agricultural production needs of tobacco, rice, sugar, and cotton farmers. The fate of these slaves was one filled with hard labor, premature deaths, and family disruptions. Central to the experiences and identities of these slaves was the way the slaveholders explained away their domination through racial ideologies that persist today in dominant discourses still rooted in slavery, including characterizations as lazy, unintelligent, mammies, and so forth (Berlin, 2003). By the time the slave trade ended, between 10 and 20 million Africans had been sold into slavery (Arthur, 2000).

Berlin (2003) asserts that the first indignity that African slaves experienced on arrival was the changing of their names. This marked the beginning of a loss of identity with and connection to the homeland from which they had been removed. The forced changes in identity that occurred through name and language loss became further acts of enslavement that, even today, mark the disconnect from historical kinship among continental Africans, African immigrants, and African (Americans) in the United States. The loss of direct ties to Africa continued through marriage between slaves from across tribal groups and between conjugal unions between female slaves and slavemasters. Consequently, cultures and traditions mixed as new identities developed as a means of survival (Johnson, Smith, & WGBH Series Research Team, 1998). What began as a means of survival soon became a new way of "comprehending and negotiating the world" (p. 89). In Césaire's (1955) words, slaves' stories became ones of "societies drained of their essence, cultures trampled underfoot, institutions undermined, lands confiscated, religions smashed, magnificent artistic creations destroyed, extraordinary possibilities wiped out" (p. 340).

In forging new identities for survival, most ascendants of African slaves now appear to be remotely identified with continental Africans as well as African immigrants. In the contexts in which contemporary African immigrants and African (Americans) find themselves today, each is reminded of who they once were and who they are becoming, as recent immigrants face the possibility of a loss of connection to the homeland as mirrored in the historical experiences of their African (American) kinfolk. As African immigrants become aware of the hierarchical racial structure that has American Blacks at the bottom of the hierarchy, they choose whether to associate or distance themselves from African (Americans) as a means of survival and identity preservation. African (Americans), on the other hand, may also respond to an unspoken hierarchy among minority ethnic groups in the United States that places African immigrants at the bottom of that hierarchy (Waters, 1994) by disassociating themselves from the newcomers.

Studies by Gibau (2005), Kusow (2006), Waters (1994), and Okpalaoka (2009a) support the ways racial and ethnic categories are expanding and challenging our traditional notions of race and ethnicity. Therefore, racial stratification cannot be overlooked as a factor in shaping the perceptions and attitudes of people in the United States (Rong & Brown, 2002a). Consequently, it is necessary to juxtapose the history of African (American) presence with that of contemporary African immigrants in order to show how time of arrival in the United States troubles the meaning of ethnic, racial, and national identities for both African immigrants and African (Americans) in the United States.

Background: History of African Immigration

Following the independence of colonized African nations in the late 1950s and 1960s, many citizens of these nations migrated to the United States to acquire the knowledge and skills needed to facilitate the necessary task of nation building in their newly formed nations (Takougang & Tidjani, 2009). This significant wave of African immigration occurred just as changes in U.S. immigration laws were ushered in by the Immigration Act of 1965 (Arthur, 2000; Takaki, 1998). Many of the African immigrants of the 1960s and 1970s returned to Africa in anticipation of the contributions they would make to their government institutions, many of which sponsored their education abroad. However, the idea of taking the helm of leadership and steering a fledgling nation in a new direction proved illusory. In just a couple of decades, corrupt leadership and unstable governments stemming from the quick ascent and descent of leadership soon led to the disillusionment and corruption that still plagues many African nations today.

The disillusionment with failed government coincided with the increasingly relaxed U.S. immigration policies of the 1970s, and the resulting political and economic chaos facilitated the admission of African refugees (among many other nationalities) who were fleeing civil wars and despotic regimes (Halter, 2007; Arthur, 2000). The 1980s also saw an increase in the number of legalized African immigrants, many of whom benefited from the immigration reforms of 1986 (the Immigration Reform and Control Act), which made it possible for undocumented Africans living in the United States to be granted legal status through an amnesty (Arthur, 2000). In a bid to reduce the number of illegal immigrants in the United States, Congress had enacted a legalization program that eventually granted legal status to 2.8 million formerly illegal immigrants (Contreras, 2002).

The 1990 Immigration Act, which raised the limit for legal immigration to 700,000 persons per year, is responsible for the most recent wave of immigrants from Africa. In addition, the Diversity Lottery Visa Program that took effect in 1995 was created to increase the number of immigrants from countries with lower immigration rates and to support the diversity goal of the

1990 Immigration Act. As a result, a large number of Africans were and continue to be admitted into the United States. According to Gordon (1998), in 1995 alone, 37% of the diversity visas awarded were to Africans. These efforts are reflected in the number of African immigrant students in our schools today and require us to address what it means for these children to be "African" in our schools and society. In addition, these totals require a closer examination of varying notions of the name African (American) and how these notions might play out in school interactions between African (American) and African immigrant students.

Being "African" American in America's Schools

> *You don't look like one, so how are you African?* (Madeline, personal interview, March 2008)

Some scholars argue that physical attributes such as African features and skin color place African immigrants at the lowest level in the racial hierarchy, and that this causes some Black immigrants to emphasize their ethnicity or nationality in an effort to de-emphasize their race as defined by American stereotypes (Bashi & McDaniel, 1997). Such arguments support statements such as the one made above by an African (American) peer of one of the West African immigrant girls in Okpalaoka's (2009a) study. It is a statement that is laden with the tensions that stem from the mutual stereotyping that occurs between African immigrant students and their African (American) peers, and it is supported by studies that have examined what it means to be "African" American in our schools (Traore, 2003, 2006; Traore & Lukens, 2006).

With the demographic changes caused by the increased diversity of our immigrant population and an increase in the number of foreign-born Black immigrants, questions about ethnic and racial identity—with regard to Black immigrants—have come to the fore. Also pushed to the fore is the resulting tension in our schools between African immigrants and their African (American) peers. Kusow (2006) shows how the increase in non-White, foreign-born immigrants to the United States draws attention to the fact that these newcomers bring national, racial, and ethnic identities with them. Therefore, researchers need to look beyond the meaning of racial categories from the historical binaries of Black and/or White to a situation of multiple, hybrid, and fluid identities (Gilroy, 1993). The ways that African immigrant children choose to identify, similar to or different from their African (American) peers, is evident in studies that have tried to address the implications of the increasing presence of African immigrants in schools (Traore, 2003, 2006; Okpalaoka, 2009a). Okpalaoka (2009a) reveals how her participants learned to wield their identity in various contexts, thereby countering the assumption that they were passive participants in their ethnic identity construction. In a study of eight African (American) and nine African students at an inner-city high school in a large city in the United States, Traore (2006) found that there was a prevalence of negative images of Africa and Africans among the African (American) student population. In another study, Traore (2003) attributed the "debilitating stereotypes" (p. 247) of Africa that her African (American) participants had to the media, which continue to perpetuate images of wild animals, Tarzan, and Africa as a "Dark Continent." Likewise, she claimed that her African participants also learned from the media that African (Americans) are violent, rude, and on welfare. She contended that the media made Africa less inviting to African (American) students by denying them "access to positive images or information about Africa and Africans" (p. 247). Traore (2006) found that the often hostile relationship between both groups of students led to each group's struggle to maintain positive ethnic and national identities. Following the intervention work she carried out to educate both groups of students about their shared heritage, Traore (2006) recommended that educators "support [students] in developing their identities free from negative stereotypes" (p. 34).

On the subject of racial identity formation among immigrant children, Rong and Brown (2002a) discovered that identities are fluid and changeable over time and in different social contexts; that Black immigrants tend to move along a continuum from a national origin identity to a hyphenated-American or American identity; and that although foreign-born Black youths are likely to choose an immigrant nationality identity (e.g., Nigerian or Jamaican), the length of time they have spent in the United States may cause them to choose a pan-national (e.g., African or Caribbean) or a pan-ethnic (Black-American) identity.

In her case study of West African immigrant girls, Okpalaoka (2009a) found that first-generation Nigerian immigrant students chose to identify as Nigerian rather than African (American) because of the negative stereotypes that they and their families associated with the latter identity. These negative stereotypes echo the dominant discourse surrounding African (Americans) as discussed earlier in this chapter. Foner (1987) and Kasinitz (1992) explain that first-generation Black immigrants tend to distance themselves from American Blacks by stressing their national origins and ethnic identities. First-generation Black immigrants may believe that accepting an immigrant nationality identity will serve as a buffer against negative stereotypes about African (Americans) (Rong & Preissle, 1998).

Okpalaoka's (2009a) study supports the notion of Black immigrants' preference for an immigrant nationality identity as demonstrated by the participant who described switching between an African (American) and Ghanaian identity, claiming to be Ghanaian in mostly Ghanaian contexts and African (American) when she was among her African (American) peers. Her decision not to disclose her Ghanaian identity in certain contexts might also be attributed to her internalization of the negative stereotypes she encountered from her African (American) peers about African peoples (Okpalaoka, 2009a). Having experienced remarks about her uncivilized African background, and wielding the characteristics of not "looking African," this young woman chose to "pass" as African (American) when it was to her benefit to do so. This situation speaks to the dominant discourses that exist between African immigrants and African (Americans) in our mutual stereotyping and that lead both groups to identify as similar to or different from the other. Understanding the position of empowerment from which this participant could name her reality and identity when and how she chose to is significant, because it could help direct the dialogue among educators, African immigrants, and African (American) students in contexts where tensions exist. Such understanding could also inform the ways Africans and African (Americans) are portrayed in school curricula.

The role of time in the ethnic identity conversations that African ascendant people engage in is not only linked to the moment and mode of their arrival in the United States as described above, but also to the matter of who can rightly claim the African in

African (American). When the African (American) peers of a first-generation immigrant girl in Okpalaoka's (2009a) case study expressed disdain of her African heritage, she responded this way:

> *What are you? You are African, because your ancestors are....I am proud to be an African 'cause I know I have a culture; you don't.* (Ekene, personal interview, March 2008)

It is significant that a young girl who had spent several years in the United States at the time of the study—centuries after slavery—would still echo the persistent stereotypes in African (American) identity that portray the African (American) as being without a history prior to the transatlantic slave trade, a history that in fact is a shared history among African ascendant peoples.

Another participant echoed the same sentiment when she shared the pride she takes in her Nigerian heritage. She felt she had an advantage over her African (American) classmates because she could speak a language other than English, and her family practiced customs and traditions that are different from those practiced in the United States. She used words like "special" and "extraordinary" to describe how she felt about the fact that she has "a background." The notion of having "a background," as a person of African ascent, appeared to be a covert comparison to African (Americans), who, according to the participants, do not have a culture or background.

The issue of naming as it relates to African identity apparently mattered to these immigrant girls and their peers, and it raises the question of whether school officials are aware of the complicated negotiations taking place, both individually and collectively, between and among the African ascendant young women. How will the heritage knowledge for all of the girls factor into school practices like curriculum and instruction? Models of culturally responsive teaching that address the need for an inclusive curriculum that meets the needs of a diverse student population like that advocated by Gay (2000), Banks (1997), and King (2005) focus on cultural responsiveness and making the invisible visible through accurate representation of history. Gay (2000) argues that "both immigrant and native-born students may...encounter prejudices, stereotyping, and racism that have negative impacts on their self-esteem, mental health and academic achievement" (p. 18). Including their histories and experiences in the curriculum may not only improve the mental health and self-esteem of these students but also help sustain conversations around what it means to educate the Black child in America.

Naming and Remembering African Relationship: Talking Back Through Transnational and Endarkened Frameworks in Education

What this discussion suggests is that scholars and educators concerned with understanding and teaching within and among the varying versions and tensions of African ascendant people (particularly as many "reclaim" our names and identities) are obligated to use research and teaching frameworks that are large and complex enough to embrace our *collective* African experiences. But the voices of these West African immigrant girls have pushed us to recognize even more deeply frameworks of endarkened[3] or Black feminism that also more deeply recognize the migratory and spiritual nature of global African identity as well. Dillard and Okpalaoka (2011) have promoted the idea of an endarkened transnational feminist epistemology that is useful. Some definitions of key terms may be important here. As previously mentioned, an *endarkened feminist epistemology* (Collins, 2000; Dillard, 2000, 2006) articulates how reality is known when based in the historical roots of global Black feminist thought. More specifically, such an epistemology embodies a distinguishable difference in cultural standpoint from mainstream (White) feminism in that it is located at the intersection/overlap of the culturally constructed notions of race, gender, class, nationality, and other identities. Perhaps most important, it arises from and informs the historical and contemporary contexts of oppression and resistance for African ascendant women. From an endarkened feminist epistemological space, we are encouraged to move away from the traditional metaphor of research as the recipe to fix a "problem" and toward a metaphor that centers in/on reciprocity and relationship between the researcher and the researched, between knowing and the production of knowledge. Thus, Dillard (2000, 2006) suggests that a more useful research metaphor of research from an endarkened feminist epistemological stance is *research as a responsibility,* answerable and obligated to the very persons and communities being engaged in the inquiry.

Our use of the term *transnational* is a literal one. We simply mean a way of looking at endarkened feminism that is beyond or through (*trans*) the boundaries of nations. But we also believe that such a look brings the possibility of a *change* in our viewpoints as scholars and teachers as well. An endarkened feminist epistemology is also an approach to teaching and research that honors the wisdom, spirituality, and critical interventions of transnational Black women's ways of knowing and being in research, with the sacred serving as a way to describe the doing of it, the way that we approach the work. Noting the distinction between spirituality and the sacred is important here. What we mean by *spirituality* is to have a consciousness of the realm of the spirit in one's work and to recognize that consciousness as a transformative force in research and teaching (Alexander, 2005; Dillard, 2006; Dillard, Abdur-Rashid, & Tyson, 2000; Fernandes, 2003; hooks, 1994; Hull, 2001; Moraga & Anzaldúa, 1981; Ryan, 2005; Wade-Gayles, 1995). Therefore, the discussions we have undertaken in this chapter are a call to action. They are a call for a transformative approach to teaching and research in relation to the dominant discourses that mark the school experiences of the Black child.

It is important here to delineate the difference between spirituality and religion, since the meanings of both are sometimes conflated. We are not advocating for formalized religion as a theoretical framework or methodological tool, but we are speaking of spirituality as a lens through which we view the relationships between and among African ascendant peoples. In contrast to the tendency of Western thought to dichotomize the material and the spiritual, we are drawing on an African spiritual concept of community and communal well-being that trumps the individualism of Western feminist thought (Steady, 1996). Dillard (2006) describes an African worldview that "is conceived as a unified spiritual whole, that is, that one's self-hood is understood and constituted as body, mind, and spirit and affirmed in relationship to both one's group and to one's creator" (p. 32). Dillard (2006) speaks to researchers and teachers having a "deep attunement" to the spiritual nature of their work and life (p. 36), or what hooks (2000) describes as experiencing "the sacred in our everyday lives...bringing to mundane tasks a quality of concentration and engagement that lifts the spirit" (p. 80). Hence, we recognize that the African spiritual concept of community and interconnectedness must be brought into the conversations we are having about African immigrants and African (Americans) in the schools. Understanding this connection, which extends beyond time and beyond the historical and geographical underpinnings of our journeys to the United States, necessitates our consideration of new methodologies with which we can explicate this knowledge to students and educators. The intended result of spiritual engagement in research and teaching is a deconstruction of hegemonic epistemologies that are still used to maintain dominant discourses that continue to divide continental Africans, African immigrants, and African (Americans).

It is also necessary to differentiate the spiritual from the sacred here. When we speak of the *sacred* in endarkened feminist research, we are referring to *the way the work is honored and embraced as it is carried out*. Said another way, work that is sacred is worthy of being held with *reverence* as it is done. The idea here is that, from endarkened or Black feminist positions, the work of teaching and research embodies and engages spirituality and is carried out in sacred ways. Thus, we believe in the notion of using both spirituality and sacredness to explore more globally the meanings, articulations, and possibilities of an endarkened feminist epistemology and viewing research as sacred, spiritual, and relevant practices of inquiry for Black women on the continent of Africa and throughout her diaspora. Mostly, we are suggesting that both spirituality and the sacred are fundamentally embedded in the very ground of inquiry, knowledge, and cultural production of Black women's everyday lives and experiences and that it is this understanding that helps us to appreciate the radical activism of Black feminism transnationally—what we see in this chapter as young girls wielding identities both to create possibilities, to structure and construct identities, and even to exclude others relationally from heritage and cultural connections. This seems particularly important to studies that focus on the role of gender among African ascendant girls, regardless of their place in the world.

We put forth here several considerations to teachers that are important to the ability to "talk back" (hooks, 1989) to dominant discourses about who African "women" (in this case, young women) are and to issues of identities and their meanings among African people through our curriculum and pedagogies. These questions suggest that as we theorize from/through endarkened transnational epistemologies, we might also shift our gaze and engagement to embrace a more sacred (reverent) understanding of our relationships with/in endarkened spaces of womanhood and feminism. In other words, we put these questions forward as representative of an endarkened transnational praxis, a way to see operationally what types of questions might move our discourses and our teaching and research forward toward an inclusive and relevant education for *all* African ascendant people. Here are the central questions.

Question 1: What does it mean to be an African woman? Endarkened transnational research acknowledges that the lives of African ascendant women are intertwined and interconnected, given our shared legacy of oppression on the African continent and in the African diaspora. As mentioned throughout, this awareness does not discount the ways that temporality shapes Black women's experiences (Okpalaoka, 2009b). Neither does this awareness discount the notion that there are variations of feminism that reflect the nuances of oppression manifested in women's specific historical, cultural, and geographical locations. The disruption of African ascendant peoples' lives through enslavement, colonization, and apartheid across temporal and geographical boundaries only serves to connect us across these boundaries. A respect for the particularities of Black women's understanding and embodiment of cultural norms, geographies, and traditions must be reflected in our research and work of inquiry in education.

If we use the examples of the young women's voices in the Okpalaoka (2009a) study that we've cited throughout this chapter, how can the knowledge of the relationship between continental Africans, African immigrants, and African (Americans) be used in our schools, and how might the knowledge of the tensions between the particular students in the study have been crafted and used by the teachers of these children? The common practice in our schools is to relegate lessons about African presence in the United States to a few pages of history or cursory mention throughout the year, except during Black History Month. Moving conversations about African ascendant peoples beyond a compensatory approach to inclusion in the curriculum (Crichlow, Goodwin, Shakes, & Swartz, 1990) whereby a few token African ascendant individuals or events are highlighted in textbooks as being representative of a people, we are calling for a broader scope of inclusion, an approach that is both emancipatory (Crichlow et al., 1990) as well as transformative (Banks, 1996). Current efforts at celebrating cultural differences through cultural fairs and exotic foods and customs are a first step, but schools cannot stop here. In addition to the curriculum revisions discussed above, schools could create forums where African and African (American) students come together to share openly about the stereotypes they hold about each other. Schools should be challenged to move beyond the food-and-festival approach to understanding other cultural and ethnic groups and focus on teaching what it means to be African or African (American), both historically and contemporarily. Transformation of ideas, school relations, and school culture might occur, not only when students see the connection between Africans who arrived in the United States as slaves and contemporary African immigrants, but also when the dominant culture and discourse begin to reflect this knowledge in school practices.

Question 2: What is the sacred nature of African women's experience? At the core of Black feminism (Collins, 2000; Steady, 1996) and endarkened feminism (Dillard, 2006) is the recognition of the expertise that we, as Black women, gain through our lived experiences and that is specific to our lived conditions. An approach to endarkened transnational feminist teaching and research is one in which the researcher/teacher and the researched are engaged in a mutually *humbling* experience, where each understands the limitations in speaking *for* the other. An endarkened transnational feminist epistemology and methodology recognizes that there are multiple experiences outside of one's own. Therefore, the role of teacher/researcher as "expert" will only serve to hinder the liberation of those with whom we engage and the cultural and spiritual knowledge that is inherently valuable to *both* of us as human and spiritual beings. The West African immigrant girls in Okpalaoka's (2009a) study reported that the use of culturally responsive pedagogy by the teachers impacted the girls' school experiences to the extent that they appreciated the coverage that Africa received in the curriculum and their role as experts on Ghana and Nigeria, which reinforced the pride they felt about their ethnic backgrounds. An endarkened transnational feminist perspective is also committed to how we "hear" the depth of meaning in the experiences of the Black children we teach. We argue here that hearing the depth of meaning in these stories is a spiritual act, and the position we assume in the hearing is sacred. The experiences of African immigrants who, perhaps for the first time, become members of a minority group upon arrival in the United States and struggle with acceptance from African (Americans), and the experiences of African (Americans) who are reminded by African immigrants of their lost connection to the continent, are legitimate experiences that should impact the ways knowledge is created and transmitted in schools. Children from both groups are experts on their own lives and should be invited as co-constructors of knowledge in the classroom experience. Only then might they begin to see the connected stories and experiences that have spanned time and geography.

Question 3: How do we recognize African community and landscapes in the work of teaching and research? The South African concept of Ubuntu ("I am because we are") and the Ghanaian (Akan) concept of Funtummireku-denkyemmireku ("We have a common destiny") embody the need to recognize the powerful and omnipresent role of community from an endarkened transnational perspective. Contrary to Western thought that seeks to elevate the individual above the community, researchers and teachers committed to an endarkened transnational feminist praxis are also committed to knowing another's stories both through telling one's own and through the sustained relationship that such dialogue requires. This is the work that researchers such as Traore (2003) and Okpalaoka (2009a) are engaged in, continually unpacking the complexities of African ascendant women's lives. From this standpoint, our work as teachers/researchers has as part of its purpose to make better conditions that may not mirror our own. In other words, while we recognize the specifics of the identities within and among African ascendant women, as long as some form of oppression is present within our collective reality, we all must engage in the struggle for freedom from oppression and full humanhood. We are in a collective struggle for liberation regardless of the specifics of our conditions. The young women whose voices we heard in this chapter, their African (American) counterparts, and all young African women join a long legacy of struggle to define ourselves in all of our complexity—and brilliance. An endarkened transnational feminist praxis works beyond self to recognize the dynamic and shifting landscapes and configurations of identity and social location of groups.

By foregrounding spirituality as a critical component of an endarkened transnational framework, we speak to its transformative power in changing lives as well as connecting all involved to a notion of humanhood that transcends the identities we choose or the names we call ourselves. Educators who are social justice practitioners can empower students through an understanding that human suffering is a global phenomenon. Rather than detach themselves from the images that they had of Africans as poor, hungry, backward, and diseased, the African (American) students in Okpalaoka's (2009a) study could have linked their struggles as African (Americans) in the United States to the social, political, and economic conditions in Africa that have led to such images. Educators could use such discussions as a springboard for action in ways that will engage the students in self-affirming and humanitarian work.

Question 4: How, within our teaching and research, are body, mind, and spirit engaged in the work? Endarkened transnational feminist research is research and teaching that makes space for mind, body, and spirit to be a part of the work. It invites the whole person of the researcher and the whole person of the researched into the work, knowing that the mind, body, and spirit are intertwined in their functions of maintaining the well-being of the individual and community. The place of the sacred in endarkened and transnational feminisms requires radical openness, especially on the part of the researcher or teacher, who understands deeply that her/his humanity is linked with that of the people s/he studies *with*. The act of sharing with those who have been silenced, marginalized, displaced (from homelands), and denied heritage knowledge (including cultural traditions, languages, and social practices) is a spiritual task that embodies a sense of humility and intimacy. Further, a sense of reciprocity is fundamental from this epistemological space, a sense that the teacher and researcher and the student and the researched are changed in the process of mutual teaching and learning the world together. As we examine the young voices in this chapter and the complicated movements and identities of African ascendant people, we must be able to imagine curricula, pedagogies, knowledges, and inquiry practices that befit the cosmopolitan (Appiah, 2006) nature of our students, the limitations of accurate historical knowledge, and the boundaries that hegemonic, racist, sexist, and xenophobic discourses have placed on the minds, bodies, and spirits of ourselves and of those whom we study and teach. In schools where classroom practice is transformative, how can teachers be open about the ways they have been impacted by systems of oppression, regardless of their identities? Rather than separate mind and spirit from the embodied self that they present in the classroom, teachers should enter the conversation as whole beings (hooks, 1994) who can empathize with their students' experiences, realizing that we are all affected by struggle and oppression, whether we are the oppressor or the oppressed (Freire, 1970). Such radical openness calls for "a commitment to a spiritual life that...requires conscious practice; a willingness to unite the way we think with the way we act" (hooks, 2000, p. 77).

The act of embracing and exploring endarkened transnational and Black feminisms also points to the fact that epistemologies, which have been marshaled in dominant discourses about African ascendant people, have still not answered the deeper, spiritual questions that undergird many cultural phenomena, the persistent social problems of equity and justice, the difficulties of community and solidarity, and the complex nature of identity and African personhood.

As we end this chapter, we reflect on the questions that have been raised here as to how a sense of the variations and tensions in African (American) identity, and the asking of new questions of dominant discourses, can inform school praxis. We have explored an endarkened transnational framework as a medium for transformative discourse, teaching, and research and as our contribution to the necessary task of confronting dominant discourses that are reflected in the tensions described in this chapter. We will end by pointing to future directions for the work ahead of us. As our schools continue to reflect the demographic makeup of the larger society, we have the responsibility of broadening our concept of what it means to educate the *Black* child today. Older definitions of African (American) may no longer hold as we consider what the processes of identity construction might mean for second-, third-, and fourth-generation African immigrants as they interact with their African (American) peers and as these peers make their own migrations in the world. New conversations will be needed, and our worldviews broadened, as we continue to address recurring issues around dominant discourses in education, especially regarding curricular reform, culturally responsive school practices, and their role in the transformative education of the Black child.

Notes

1. A writer uses parentheses to denote or mark off explanatory or qualifying remarks. We used them here to identify those persons of African ascent who were born to parents who are direct ascendants of Africans brought to the United States through the transatlantic slave trade. This representational move is to highlight the often-ignored African heritage connections that still exist between African (Americans) and those throughout the African continent and the diaspora.

2. The data used in this article derive mostly from personal and group interviews, conducted from February to March 2008, of four adolescent girls of Nigerian and Ghanaian ascent. Additional sources of data are the journals kept by the participants during the study.

3. By using the term "endarkened" in endarkened feminist epistemology, Dillard (2000, 2006) articulates how reality is known when placed in the context of the historical roots of global Black feminist thought. It is a term that plays on the concept of enlightenment while distinguishing itself from mainstream (White) feminism in its location at the intersections of race, gender, class, nationality, and other identities.

Chapter 2

On Naming

Contestations and Nuanced Complexities in Naming the Feminist Spirit

The previous chapter examined the tensions and variations that accompany the issue of African identity and how asking new questions of dominant discourses around race, ethnicity, and African identity can inform school praxis. In order to move the discourse forward, the chapter explored an endarkened transnational framework as a medium for transformative discourse, teaching, and research. In keeping with the forward thinking and upward mobility inherent in the term "African ascendant," this chapter will extend the dialogue to include conversations about appropriate research methodology and why we must turn our focus and energy to the complexities of naming the work that African ascendant women are doing on behalf of one another.

When I embarked on my study of adolescent girls of Nigerian and Ghanaian ascent to understand how they negotiated their ethnic identities as young Black girls growing up in immigrant homes in the United States (Okpalaoka, 2009b), my goal was to provide a way of looking at Black women's lives not as a monolithic entity, but as lives that hold some commonality of experience with struggle and oppression. Situated within a multicultural feminist framework, the intent of that study was to highlight the voices of the girls whose stories were absent from the literature on Black immigration and Black ethnic identity development. I chose to work from a Black feminist epistemology because I believed at the time that it was most fitting for the study, considering the possibilities of their raced and gendered experiences as Black females in the United States. At the conclusion of the study I began to reflect on epistemologies that might even more clearly capture the transnational spaces that Black women occupy in the diaspora and the appropriate methodologies that would have fit studies such as mine. This search led to the furthering of an endarkened transnational feminism that speaks to the complexities of Black and endarkened feminisms and epistemologies existent on the continent of Africa, in the United States, and the African diaspora (Alexander, 2005; Dillard & Okpalaoka, 2011).

As discussed in the previous chapter, central to the findings of the study with the immigrant girls were feelings of inferiority rooted in negative stereotypes about Africa. This also marked some of the interactions of many of the participants with their peers. As an African ascendant scholar who came of age in postcolonial and post-independent Nigeria, I, too, have encountered these same negative stereotypes and the resulting feelings of inferiority, both in the United States and in Nigeria. Beyond our shared experiences with the residual effects of colonialism and the trauma on our psyche as a people who continue to wrestle with the notion of African inferiority is the fact that the girls in my study and I live in the United States where, as Black women with ties to the continent, we are also implicated in the discourses surrounding who we are as Black women. These discourses question whether our struggles with interlocking oppressions, like our sisters everywhere, can be similarly named, and what frameworks best suit the work we do or the work that is done about us.

The goal of this chapter is to explore the connections between my experiences as a Black female researcher raised in postcolonial Nigeria and the experiences of Black women in the diaspora. This is not an exhaustive comparison or compilation of the various identities that African ascendant women assume in the world, nor am I claiming that my experiences or those of the girls in my study represent the experiences of all Black women. But I argue that connections are apparent in our experiences with racism, classism, sexism, and other forms of power and privilege which, though distinctive to our geographical and historical locations, still resonate *wherever* Black women are situated.

I have come to a belated yet critical realization that the study that I continue to conduct with the girls and others like them calls for a more global perspective in looking at Black women's experiences with identity and struggle in the African diaspora, regardless of how the work is named. Therefore, I will begin by addressing the contestations around the issue of appropriate naming of the feminist spirit in the work of and about Black women. Then I will promote the possibilities of Black feminist, endarkened feminist, and African feminist epistemologies as viable lenses through which the narratives included here can be viewed. Finally, I will recommend a transnational endarkened feminist epistemology (introduced in the previous chapter) and corresponding methodologies that embrace all of the above feminisms by situating them globally in a move that might begin to capture the ways African ascendant women "are" in the world today. These narratives will describe how I enter into this discourse with a brief look at my earliest experiences with the residual effects of colonial rule in Nigeria. I will also include the narratives of the young girls' negotiation of identities as they try to understand what it means to be Black women with feet firmly planted on two continents—Africa and North America. Using our collective narratives as data sources, I hope to demonstrate that there are recurring themes in the experiences of African ascendant women and the ways these experiences impact the work that we choose to do and how we choose to do it.

Naming the Feminist Spirit

Requiring a consensus as to what labels most succinctly capture the work that African ascendant women are doing around the globe, contemporary contestations about the issue of naming and "appropriate" feminist terminology may divert our attention from doing critical, urgent, and collaborative work. Some argue whether the term Black feminism (Collins, 2000) captures the experiences of African ascendant women in the diaspora for whom post- and neo-colonialism may trump gender, race, and class as the issues that are of foremost relevance to our communities (Nnaemeka, 1998; Steady, 1981, 2004). Other scholars call for a more appropriate terminology such as Africana womanism (Hudson-Weems, 1993), which, in contrast to Black and African feminisms, captures the reality of African women's struggles by not according gender primary status in struggles for a just and humane society (Hudson-Weems, 1998). While the latter argument is that African feminism identifies with White feminism in its retention of the feminist label (and therefore embraces the latter's assumptions of a universal womanhood) (Hudson-Weems, 1998), African feminists such as Nnaemeka (1998), Ogundipe-Leslie (1994), Aidoo (1998), and Steady (1981) choose to focus on the dynamics of collective efforts on the African continent to ensure that all persons, not just women, are treated with dignity and respect. Speaking of then-President Nyerere of Tanzania's model for women's participation in political and nation-building activities, Ladner (1981) critiqued the ensuing dissent that a women's liberation movement was being encouraged and that this would prove to be a divisive rather than a uniting force in Tanzania. Others argued that the creation of a special political group for women was still a form of discrimination that relegated women to working with each other on women's issues only. Echoing African feminists such as Nnaemeka (1998), Ogundipe-Leslie (1994), Aidoo (1998), and Steady (1981), Ladner argues that the women's movement, rather than something to be viewed in the context of women's liberation, was a call for an equal opportunity for *all* able-bodied Tanzanians to participate in nation building.

Similarly, feminist scholars and proponents of women's rights in the Middle East and North Africa are drawing from international standards of human rights to argue for a reformation of family laws that continue to keep women subjugated (Moghadam, 2008). By leaning on international standards of human rights, feminist scholars from the Middle East and North Africa are asserting that *all* human beings, regardless of gender, must be treated equally before the law.

> Their arguments are based on principles related to human rights, international conventions, the global women's rights agenda and an Islamic feminist re-reading of the religious sources. They also have appealed to governments to make their domestic policies conform to international conventions, such as the Convention on the Elimination of All Forms of Discrimination Against Women (CEDAW) and the Beijing Platform for Action. (Moghadam, 2008, p. 12)

Whether women's rights issues are being taken up in the Caribbean (see Pinto, 2010, on the role of the diasporic slave trade and colonial indentured servitude of "coolies" in racial tensions in Trinidad), or in Latin America as exemplified by the Latin American and Caribbean Feminist Encuentros (encounters) which, for over 2 decades, has provided a forum for dialogue around issues of identities and practices distinctive to the varied feminisms of the region (Alvarez et al., 2002), the fact remains that women around the globe—especially those who claim a connection to Africa—are also connected by their experiences with subjugation, regardless of the form or manifestation of the particular oppressions women face in these contexts. Hudson-Weems (1998) asserts that a collectivity of struggle with and for the entire Black community in the diaspora will lead to the restoration of dignity not only to African ascendant people, but to all humanity. This collectivity, defined by Hudson-Weems (1998) as a working together of African ascendant people to confront oppression, requires us to show how our experiences in the diaspora—with enslavement, colonization, apartheid, nationalism, religion, race, class, and gender discrimination—illustrates that "any argument arising between us would be silenced as we [turn] our combined energy to scrutinize an oncoming foe" (Walker, 2006, p. 4). The common foes in this case are racism, classism, sexism, and other forms of domination and oppression that seek to keep subjugated not only women but all people of African ascendancy.

Collins (2000) also alludes to these naming contestations by offering new insights into what she calls a "global matrix of domination" (p. 228) and by demonstrating that "all contexts of domination incorporate some combination of intersecting oppressions" (p. 228). She encourages us to consider and place Black women's experiences with struggle and oppression in a global context. In the preface to the second edition of her *Black Feminist Thought: Knowledge, Consciousness, and the Politics of Empowerment*, Collins (2000) reveals how rethinking Black women's empowerment led to her own incorporation of new themes in the 2000 edition, one of which cautions U.S. Black women to continue to struggle not only for their own empowerment but for the empowerment of women of African ascent everywhere. She further recognizes that there are "commonalities that join women of African [ascent] as well as differences that emerge from our diverse national histories" (p. xi). Recognizing the diversity of histories and experiences, Collins (2000) argues that we must look beyond particular organizations of matrices of domination to the "universality of intersecting oppressions as organized through diverse local realities" (p. 228). The idea of a "universality of intersecting oppressions" acknowledges the particular experiences of the girls in my study, my own experiences, and the experiences of the African ascendant women as we continue to struggle with oppressions that intersect along racial, cultural, gender, class, and national lines.

In the same vein, hooks (1994) speaks about the influence of Freire's writings that have allowed her "to place the politics of racism in the United States in a global context wherein [she] can see [her] fate linked with that of colonized Black people everywhere struggling to decolonize, to transform society" (p. 53). Elaborating on the influence of Freire's work on her own, hooks (1994) recounts how her introduction to Freire's writings and "global understanding of liberation struggles" (p. 47) coincided with her search for a language that allowed her to question the politics of domination not only in the United States but with marginalized people beyond U.S. shores. There is a link between the works of hooks (1994), Freire (1970/2000), and Collins (2000) in the ways they address the broader struggles not just of Black people but people all over the globe. They speak conceptually of domination and oppression and the possibilities of liberation that transcend gender, nation, or state.

So, rather than be misconstrued as a call for a monolithic African ascendant womanhood or a set of theories in response to the inequities we experience, this chapter focuses on the notion that the interlocking oppressions that Black women face in the diaspora, regardless of the nuanced variations of said oppressions, serve as connectors to a unifying goal for liberation and empowerment. We must learn from Dillard (2006) that our "ways of being (our culture), [our] ways of knowing (our theory), and our ways of leading (culturally engaged) are...a place from which we center and make sense of our work..." as African ascendant women (p. 11). Therefore, my identity and my experiences as a researcher of African ascent impact every aspect of my work—from my choice of research topics to the questions I ask. I am also a mother who is raising her children in a Nigerian immigrant home in the United States and who observes the contextual negotiation of their identities as Black children in the United States. In this way, I acknowledge that there was a personal agenda to the study on which this chapter is based. The reasons for this study also include my experiences as a young woman who was born in the United States, raised in Nigeria, and who, upon returning to the United States as an adult, has experienced the complexities of intra- and interracial interactions and how these impact the identities I assume contextually.

I have chosen to approach the narratives in this chapter from Black feminist (Collins, 2000) and endarkened feminist (Dillard, 2006) frameworks, since they encompass theoretical interpretations of Black women's reality by those who live it (Collins, 2000).

Thus, my lived experience is the location from which I will be theorizing about my life. Black feminist thought, like other oppositional knowledges, argues for intersecting oppressions as a critical social theory that "supports broad principles of social justice that transcend U.S. Black women's particular needs" (Collins, 2000, p. 22). Endarkened feminist epistemology, as articulated by Dillard (2006), not only examines Black women's reality based in the historical roots of Black feminist thought, but also views research as a practice of responsibility that is accountable to the communities within which we work.

I will also discuss my experiences from an African feminist perspective because of the specific role that neo-colonialism and post-colonialism have played in the experiences of African women. Nnaemeka (1998) argues that a meaningful description of African feminism requires a closer look at the African environment. She says that African feminism "has a life of its own that is rooted in the African environment" (p. 9) and that "the contemporary African woman is a creation of historical and current forces that are simultaneously internally generated and externally induced" (p. 14). These forces, which include westernization, Christianity, Islamization, neo-colonialism, and post-colonialism, along with culture, race, class, and gender, form the matrices of domination/oppression for African women.

By situating this chapter within Black, African, and endarkened feminist epistemologies, I am speaking to the relationship that exists among these epistemologies and the ways that the experiences of women like me, the girls in my study, and other African ascendant women can simultaneously be interpreted through Black, African, and endarkened feminist lenses, depending on the space we occupy at a given time. Clearly, there are distinctions in the experiences of African ascendant women in the diaspora with systems of oppression: Collins (2000) argues that the universality of experiences with oppression vary from one social, cultural, historical, and geographical context to another. Dillard and Okpalaoka (2011) also argue that in spite of the similarity in the contexts and manifestations of domination across the diaspora, we must recognize the role that history and temporality have played in the forms of oppression that Black women confront. History and time have not only determined whether Black women have been subjugated by race, class, gender, culture, colonization, or any other forms of domination, but also which of these forms of oppression have dominated in each context. Therefore, African feminists such as Nnaemeka (1998) and Steady (1981) have suggested the notions of "a common ground" (Nnaemeka, 1998, p. 3) and "the power of sisterhood" (Nnaemeka, 1998, p. 4) that respect the particular nuances of Black women's experiences, while Black feminists such as Collins (2000), Dillard (2006), and hooks (1994) extend the notion of commonality by challenging us to focus on the common themes of struggle and spirituality shared by Black women within Africa, the United States, and the diaspora.

Recognizing that mainstream discourses surrounding multiple epistemologies have not captured the complexities or the commonalities of Black, endarkened, and African feminisms, Dillard and Okpalaoka (2011) proposed a *globally focused* or *globally situated* Black or endarkened feminism that recognizes and embraces the collective diversity of Black women's experiences as a necessary departure from the contestations surrounding previous definitions of "Black feminism," "womanism," "Africana womanism," and/or "Third World feminism." According to Dillard and Okpalaoka (2011), these definitions may no longer hold as bridges across our differences in paradigms. The paradigm we propose is an endarkened transnational one that revisits what it means to be Black women beyond the typical understandings of national boundaries to all of the spaces that African ascendant women occupy in the diaspora. An endarkened transnational feminism not only recognizes that Black women in the diaspora can place their experiences within a context of struggle against systems of oppression and exploitation, but it also recognizes that Black women's experiences with struggles are engaged within a context of spirituality that enables Black women to survive and even to thrive, regardless of what forms of oppression are operating in their particular context. It is from/within such a space, one that is endarkened and transnational, that my narrative and those of the others begin.

Re-membering: The Beginnings

To demonstrate the connection between the issues of naming the feminist spirit and the global contexts in which Black women live and struggle, I will situate my own experiences as an African ascendant scholar. When Collins (2000) persuades us to consider the global nature of Black women's experiences and the factors that have shaped these experiences, she also makes a strong historical connection between Black women's experiences with slavery and colonialism. African feminist Oyeronke Oyewumi (1997) has already urged us to extend our understanding of colonization beyond the period of actual African colonization by recognizing that the period of the Atlantic slave trade and African colonization were one continuous process manifesting in different forms and spanning temporal dimensions. Therefore, the oppression of continental African women, even in their migrations to other parts of the globe, must be understood within the context of the lingering effects of colonialism.

Since I came of age at the end of colonial rule in Nigeria, my knowledge of colonial Nigeria came mostly from historical and literary texts that remained in use in Nigerian schools long after colonial rule ended. Our history books introduced me to the "outsiders" who came to save us from ourselves. These texts taught me that we were an "uncivilized" people waiting to be discovered and redeemed. Therefore, it was from the school texts that I learned who the White man said the African was, always in contrast to himself. Frantz Fanon captures this imposition of identity by the colonizer in his essay "The Fact of Blackness" (1967).

> The Black man among his own in the twentieth century does not know at what moment his inferiority comes into being through the other....In the first chapter of the history that the others have compiled for me, the foundation of cannibalism has been made eminently plain in order that I may not lose sight of it....And so it is not I who make meaning for myself, but it is the meaning that was already there, pre-existing, waiting for me....(pp. 110, 120, 134)

It was not until I became an English major in college that I was introduced to pre-colonial, colonial, and post-colonial literary works by African writers such as Achebe (1960; 1966; 1969; 1975; 2000) and Armah (1969, 1973), who richly captured traditional African cultures, the disintegration of African societies caught in a war between Western and traditional paradigms, and the enduring effects of colonialism on the psyche of the people. Although the notion of an uncivilized African who was intellectually, socially, culturally, and spiritually inferior to the European colonizer was the impetus for the partition and colonization of Africa, it is also a notion that has lingered in the minds of the former colonizer and the colonized.

Colonization, whether in Africa or elsewhere, requires that the colonized be mentally dominated (Fanon, 1967). On the subject of mental colonization, Petersen (1995) argues that colonization is not just a geographical phenomenon, but also one that is simultaneously economic, intellectual, educational, and mental, and which ultimately leaves internal colonialism in its wake long after colonialism *de jure* is over. It is no surprise that British colonial influence is still pervasive in the lives of the Nigerian people today, since the oppressed, once they have been successfully convinced that their indigenous ways are inferior, usually take on the oppressors' modus operandi. In *Pedagogy of Hope*, Freire (1992) describes this process as "interiorization of the dominant ideology by the dominated" (p. 46), and in *Pedagogy of the Oppressed* (2000), he describes it as "self-deprecation which derives from [the oppressed's] internalization of the opinion the oppressors hold of them" (p. 45).

My earliest recollection of witnessing what I later understood to be the residual effect of mental and intellectual colonization begins about 13 years after Nigeria's independence from Britain. There was a family day celebration going on at the research institute where my father worked. When I realized that some of the kids in attendance were enjoying ice cream treats, I went to the counter to get some. The man behind the counter told me that the ice cream was for the children of senior staff members only. I must have been around 6 or 7 years old at the time, but I knew, even at that age, that we qualified to be recipients of the special treat. I also knew that this man had reached the conclusion he had because my sister and I did not fit a certain image he had constructed in his head. I reported the incident to my father, who returned to the counter with me to intervene. He introduced himself to the bartender, making sure he conveyed his status at the institute, and requested that we be served ice cream like the other children. I remember the childlike satisfaction of knowing that my father was important enough for us to get ice cream that hot day.

This is my earliest recollection of confronting some form of discrimination because I did not fit a certain category. In other words, the privilege of enjoying an ice cream treat was not typically available to a Nigerian child in the particular context in which this incident transpired. In an institution that was run predominantly by Western expatriates, the assumption by the bartender was that I did not look like one of the expatriate children and therefore did not qualify to be a recipient of the ice cream. I did not consider my sense of entitlement in terms of the privilege I benefitted from at that time, but it was apparent that even in what appeared to be "winning" in the face of discrimination, my privileged experience was atypical. This story exemplifies ways that hierarchies can still exist, even in the intersectionalities of our identities and oppressions.

It was not until I had to write this chapter that I reminded my father of this incident. Here I share my father's version of the context within which the ice cream story is set, a version that extends my own. The research institute was established by several international organizations. Consequently, the institute's senior positions were mostly staffed by expatriates. My father was one of only two Nigerians among the senior staff rank because of their advanced degrees, which earned them reluctant admission into the senior staff club. In other words, my father and his colleague were the first two Nigerians to integrate the all-White senior staff club. My father recounts how he and his colleague later fought for the staff club to be opened up to other Nigerians who were research assistants and who were all university graduates.

The resistance to the demands for integration eventually gave way to the opening up of club membership to everyone in the scientific management rank. This was the backdrop to the events of the day I asked the bartender for ice cream. Apparently, he was not yet aware that the staff club had been integrated, hence his refusal to serve my sister and me some ice cream. I now understand that the bartender's perception of the staff hierarchy at the institute and his decision about which staff children deserved to be served ice cream as an example of mental colonization.

I also came to understand that mental colonization is not confined to the locale in which the colonized dwells. Even in migration to other locales, the formerly colonized may still carry residual notions of inferiority to their new settlement. This mindset becomes a sort of baggage that, if unexamined, determines the lens through which the formerly colonized see themselves and others. Just as Reid (1938) argued about the foreign-born Negro long ago, contemporary African immigrants in the United States also find that, though we have changed geographical location, we continue to be subsumed by the inter- and intra-racial processes into which we are thrust upon arrival in our new homeland.

Connections: "I am because we are" [1]

In a pilot study carried out during my graduate studies that examined the school experiences of African immigrant girls in predominantly White, suburban schools, one of the participants (a second-generation immigrant girl of Ghanaian ascent) kept referring to herself as "slow." This was in contrast to her Ghanaian-born brother, who had been partially educated in Ghana before migrating to the United States and who was excelling in school. What was striking was her surprise that her Ghanaian-educated brother was succeeding in a U.S. school.

> Even though I don't really understand how, my brother, you know...some people would think since my brother was born and raised in Africa...his grades wouldn't be as good...and how I was born and raised in America and I took the classes all my life...how I would get such, you know, kind of almost low grades. (personal interview, March 2006)

This young woman's statements suggest that she may have internalized negative perceptions of Africans and African education as being of inferior quality, and this framed her comparisons of education for African and U.S. education. Her statements indicated that she was clearly surprised that her brother, who was partially educated in Ghana, performed better academically than she, who was born and educated in the United States.

Why did this young woman expect that a U.S. education would be more challenging than an African one? Why did she believe that her Ghanaian-born brother would be the product of an inferior education based solely on the locality of his initial educational experience? At what point do the oppressed begin to believe that their ways are inferior to those of their oppressors? These questions cannot be answered without a look at the effects of colonialism and oppression on the psyche of the oppressed and the subtle yet thorough indoctrination of the colonized, most often through colonial or the oppressor's education. Soyinka-Airewele (2005) references this phenomenon in her explanation of the purpose of colonial-type education, which she argues was to "further the exploitation of the colonial peoples and to teach students to reject their own culture and realities, while seeing a Western education as a status symbol" (pp. 111–112). The resulting self-deprecation is a result of the oppressed people's internalization of the oppressor's opinions of them as incapable and inferior (Freire, 2000).

Colonization requires that the colonized be mentally dominated, because the purpose of colonial education is to educate the people to serve the needs of the oppressor. In order to achieve this purpose, the master needs to convince the people that their way of being and doing things is barbaric, primitive, and uncivilized. After colonialism has ended, the liberated people begin to associate the oppressors' ways of work, dress, personal care, speech, and intellectual ability with "the right way" or "the civilized way" of being and doing. Freire (2000) contends that the oppressed "almost never realize...that they, too, 'know things' they have learned in their relations with the world and with other women and men" (p. 45).

The findings of my study of first- and second-generation immigrant girls of West African ascent in the United States and how they learn to construct their ethnic identities revealed several processes of internalization of the "right way of being" (Okpalaoka, 2009a). One of the participants, a recent Nigerian immigrant to the United States, explained her reasons for adopting silence as a survival tool in the classroom. The young girl's narrative revealed that her response to the perceived reaction of her peers and teachers to her accented speech limited her classroom participation. She was very conscious of her speech and, although she did not make any direct attribution of her silence to any particular stereotypes she had experienced, it is likely that there were covert reactions to her accented speech that made her believe it was something to be ashamed of. It seemed that her peers' and teachers' speech were the norm against which she measured hers and concluded that her accent was inferior.

> My teacher had problems with me, because I [didn't] really talk, 'cause when I talk they might say that, "Oh, she talks differently." I really didn't feel like talking, 'cause everyone spoke differently and the teacher, he speaks—like, I was used to people talking a little bit slower than they are—but he was so sharp. He spoke a lot of stuff. I really didn't understand what he was saying 'cause he was speaking so fast. (personal interview, 2/11/08)

Waters (1994) maintains that an accent "is usually a clear and unambiguous signal to other Americans that [the immigrant] is foreign born" (p. 798). In a study that was designed to investigate the relationship between level of accentedness and the characteristics attributed to the speaker, Ryan, Carranza, and Moffie (1977) discovered that accented speech is negatively stereotyped and that the more accented the speech, the stronger the stereotype. So those in attendance were denied this young girl's contribution to the classroom experience just because *she* believed she sounded different from her peers. And she missed the opportunity to create and name the world as she experienced or lived it.

Another study participant, a second-generation Ghanaian immigrant, described her experiences with mostly negative stereotypes about Africans as being poor, dirty, and diseased. She appeared to have internalized some of the negative stereotypes about Africans as evidenced by her response to my question as to what ethnic identity she chooses. Her internalization of these stereotypes seemed to be the source of the fear she felt about revealing her African heritage. When I asked how she introduced herself to people, she said:

> I'll say I'm Ghanaian. Sometimes I like to hide because I'm scared to see what people might, you know, be like, "Eww, you're from Africa?" But now I'm just used to it. (personal interview, February 2008)

She stated further:

> When I'm usually in a Ghanaian community I can fit myself in, but when there's a variety of African Americans, I just be like, "Oh, I'm an African American," instead of I'm just an *ordinary* Ghanaian [emphasis mine]. (personal interview, February 2008)

And:

> Sometimes, I feel like I don't want to be an African or Ghanaian at all. I just want to be just a *regular* person instead of just being a Ghanaian [emphasis mine]. (personal interview, February 2008)

This young girl's use of the words "ordinary" to describe her Ghanaian heritage and "regular" to describe an African American identity that was preferable to a Ghanaian identity was significant because she appeared to understand when it was favorable for her to identify as African American. Her choice of an African American over an African identity appeared to be contextual and implied a not-often-discussed racial and ethnic hierarchy in the United States between African Americans and African immigrants. She seemed to have picked up on this seemingly invisible or unspoken hierarchical structure, which too often places African Americans above Africans in the United States. This means that there may be contexts in which choosing one identity over the other may privilege the person who is making the choice. In this case, the African was the "other" with whom this participant did not want to associate in some contexts. By refusing to disclose her Ghanaian heritage in certain contexts, this young girl's claim to being African American stood in opposition to the stereotypical comments she had heard her peers express about Africans. Her claim to an African American identity could also be read as internalization of the stereotypes she had heard about Africa.

Going back to early representations of Africans in colonial literature, Chinua Achebe's (1958/2000) critique of colonial misrepresentations of Nigeria and its people include Joyce Cary's book *Mister Johnson*, which was widely acclaimed in the United States and in the U.K., in spite of its portrayal of "grinning," "senseless" savages. The portrayal of Africans as uncivilized people has justified—and still justifies—most dehumanizing assaults on and outside the continent, be they through slavery or colonization. Freire (1970) has also argued that the oppressor needs to dehumanize the oppressed in order to justify the oppression.

One of the ways that oppression manifests itself is to convince the oppressed that the oppressor's ways are superior. Wakefield and Hudley (2007) argue that

> members of minority groups in a hierarchical multiethnic society like the United States must consider the extent to which they will sustain a unique group identity, identify with characteristics that afford success in the dominant society, and negotiate their relationships with others similarly situated as minorities in relation to the powerful dominant group. (p. 148)

Because she may have bought into the unspoken hierarchy among minority ethnic groups in the United States that places African immigrants at the bottom of the ethnic ladder (Waters, 1994; Rong & Brown, 2002a), this young woman appeared to understand where Black Africans are situated in comparison to

African Americans and the dominant group and chose to disassociate herself from an African identity. Other studies (Waters, 1994) have also shown how study participants chose to "pass" as Black Americans when they recognized the higher status Black Americans enjoyed in comparison to foreign-born and second-generation Haitian immigrants.

I understand this recognition of social stratification too well, as I am reminded of my first job at a department store when I first arrived in the United States. I often agonized about speaking out with my accented speech in group settings, even when I had brilliant ideas to share. I was conscious of the difference ascribed to my way of speaking, and I did not want to stand out from the rest of the group. Having being asked too many times to "say that again," I clearly understood that my accented speech was not the norm and only served to provoke negative impressions or judgments about me and/or my intellectual capabilities. I also understood that the norm that had been set before I got to the United States was one that required me to understand that non-accented speech was a goal that I should strive to attain in order to belong. Rong and Brown (2002a), who have done significant work on the socialization, culture, and identities of Black immigrant children, also argue that having African ancestry or African phenotypical features places Black immigrants at "the lowest level of the racial hierarchy" (p. 253). This notion of subordinate positioning based on African ancestry marks my experiences and the experiences of the girls in my study and serves to connect us to the larger issues of oppression that Black women struggle with everywhere. It is a notion that transcends the feminist labels we choose and the names we call ourselves.

So when Hudson-Weems (1998) connects the collectivity of struggle of the Black community in the diaspora to the struggle for the restoration of dignity to African ascendants, she is actually challenging us to see how acts of subordination rob us all of our humanity. Determined efforts to subjugate African ascendant people—whether in the United States, on the African continent, or in the diaspora—occur in all the transnational spaces that we occupy and, therefore, must be examined from an endarkened transnational feminist perspective. When we understand the restoration of dignity to African ascendant peoples, then we also understand the rationale for transforming research methodologies and methods that dignify as they liberate.

Transforming and Transformed Epistemologies

I can now make the connection between myself, the girls in my study, the man who refused to serve me ice cream many years ago, and the larger, interrelated issues of colonization and feminism. It appears that the girls, the bartender, and I learned well that there is a standard way of being, doing, and speaking that has been designated by dominant groups as acceptable. Even when the rejection of our difference is subtle, we pick up on the reactions to our being. Just as I knew that I did not fit a norm when the guy behind the counter refused to serve me ice cream, my study participants and I also knew when our accented speech did not fit the norm. We see this clearly in the young girl who was surprised that her African-educated brother could excel in U.S. schools, and in the one who had mastered the art of identity switching from an African to an African American identity when the claiming of an African identity was a source of shame for her.

Like other Black female researchers (hooks, 1981, 1994; Lorde, 1984; Ogundipe-Leslie, 1994; Nnaemeka, 1998), my personal experiences and my experiences as a researcher with the residual effects of colonialism and oppression and the consequent feelings of inferiority and shame have helped shape my work. I "invoke [my] own concrete experiences and those of other women and communities of color in [my] selection of topics for investigation and for the methodologies that [I] engage" (Collins, 1990, p. 23). I have attempted to examine the complexities of Black, African, and endarkened feminisms and epistemologies and use them as a launching pad from which I advance an endarkened transnational feminism. My choice of endarkened transnational epistemology and corresponding methodology hinges on a desire to challenge and transform the thinking processes of people who have learned well from past and present oppressors that they are not worth much except as defined by the oppressor. Whether in being, doing, or in choice of a research paradigm, Dillard (2006) calls for educational research that truly transforms through transformed epistemologies. As Dillard (2006) argues, I cannot separate my research methodologies from the historical and cultural situations in which I work. She further explains that "a research paradigm becomes the way in which scholars, teachers, and thinkers articulate their sense of life around them, make sense and order of the universe" (p. 32). Therefore, I draw from an epistemology that is endarkened, transnational, Black, feminist, and African, one that centers the right of being and becoming on Black women across the globe.

What, then, would transformative methodology look like for a study anchored in transformative epistemologies, in naming our realities as we know them as Black women? First of all, it would be *a methodology that allows the silenced voices of oppressed women to be heard.* Although the notion of voice is a fundamental Black (Collins, 2000; hooks, 1981), African (Nnaemeka, 1998; Aidoo, 1998), and indigenous (Tuhiwai-Smith, 1999) feminist work, the consideration I offer here is especially pertinent to the work we do with West African immigrant girls because of the role that traditional African gender expectations have played in our experiences. Although African immigrant families in the United States have changed geographical location, some traditional gender expectations still persist. The families of the participants in my study hoped the girls would maintain a connection to their ethnic heritage through the practice of traditional gender roles like cooking and keeping house. One of the girls captured this very succinctly in her remark that "Girls cook and boys watch T.V."

A transformative epistemology that seeks to give voice to women must acknowledge that the silencing of women's voices exists on a continuum. Therefore, it is important that researchers understand the processes and structures that have led to the silencing of women's voices in the particular context in which they work. Only then can we understand how to go about making space for oppressed voices. As scholars and researchers, we must consider that there are parts of the globe where African ascendant women's voices are silenced on matters in which their sisters in other locations have gained considerable ground. Therefore the notion of silencing may take on varied meanings in varied cultural contexts.

With the understanding that the voice of the oppressed is usually subsumed by the oppressor's voice, which seeks to remind her of her subordination to the oppressor, the space for voice could be created through the use of participant journals and other writings like poetry or prose for data collection. The participants' voices must also be foregrounded through the use of their narratives as data source. An examination of traditional scholarship reveals that

Black women's experiences have been excluded from traditional scholarship (Collins, 2000), and Black women's need for self-definition and traditional sites of knowledge include "alternative" sites such as music, narratives, daily conversations, and so on, as locations for articulating core themes of Black feminist consciousness (Bell Scott, 1994; Collins, 2003; Dillard, 2006). When researchers create the space for these voices to be heard, we begin to practice what Julia Cameron (1999) calls writing that "rights things" (p. 38).

The young girl in my study who had been silenced in school because of others' reactions to her accented speech turned out to be very vocal during the personal and group interviews. In the research journals that were provided to the participants for the purpose of finding and expressing their voices during the study, the same girl commented: "I really enjoyed the interview and it is the first time I feel safe to open up to someone." This comment assured me that she felt heard for the first time in a long while. By inviting her and the other participants to share their stories as a means of foregrounding the stories of other girls like them, this young woman appeared to have found her voice. The consideration for a methodology that helps oppressed women find their voice extends the arguments advanced by scholars like Tuhiwai-Smith (1999) that "different worldviews and alternative ways of coming to know, and of being..." (p. 74) are still legitimate and must be brought to the fore regardless of how the speech that brings forth this knowledge sounds to the listener.

Collins (1990) attests to the empowerment that comes when Black women intellectuals re-articulate the lives of other Black women. By recognizing that Black women can be theorists, Black women intellectuals can offer other Black women a distinct view of themselves and their world that differs from that held by the dominant group (Omi & Winant, 1986). I believe that this young woman's realization of her voice supports the need for a methodology that creates safe spaces and empowers African ascendant women to speak out. The knowledge of this young girl's experience with silence, which stemmed from her accented speech, might help educators seek out ways to include the voices of students like her in classroom discourse.

Second, a methodology for work that will transform the lives of African ascendant women regardless of their location is *a method-*

ology that is participatory in nature. It is a methodology that will promote a research experience in which the researcher and the researched are engaged in a mutual commitment to the well-being of the community, a process that Dillard (2006) describes as incorporating "alternative epistemological truths" (p. 2) that require researchers' commitment to the communities they study. This commitment and responsibility of the researcher to the researched is reflected in Dillard's (2006) call for "a more useful research metaphor arising from an endarkened epistemology... [which is] research as a responsibility, answerable and obligated to the very persons and communities being engaged in the inquiry" (p. 5).

Mbilinyi (1984) cautions against elite African women scholars' adoption of the conceptual approaches established by Western liberal scholars, but encourages scholars who work with women on the African continent or in the diaspora to develop frameworks defined by the reality of the historical and cultural practices of the people. It is important that researchers who seek to engage in participatory research with African ascendant women understand the hierarchical structure of authority in the contexts they study. For example, traditional African cultural practices include the value of respect for elders and those in authority, whether we speak of parents, older relatives, adults in the community, or even the researcher. I contend that this could interfere with the process of participatory research in which the researcher is accorded a status of being the *only* authority figure, one who is all-knowing. Some knowledge of the dynamics of societal relationships and their inherent hierarchical structure in the context within which we work is necessary, since it will determine the extent to which the researcher may seek to narrow the authority divide.

The girls in my study also shared their parents' expectations that they respect adults in their community and school. They were expected to extend to other adults and authority figures the same respect that they accord their parents. As a researcher who has cultural knowledge of the ways the notion of respect could impact the research process, I translated this knowledge into several choices I made throughout the study. In the end, a methodology that is participatory is one that chooses not to reinforce the notion of the researcher as expert and all-knowing and the participant as subject to the researcher. Such a methodology will not recreate models of the superior versus the inferior inherent in the oppressive relationships from which the participants seek to liberate themselves. Here are some examples.

How the researcher presents herself is critical to the interview process (Fontana & Frey, 2003). I deliberately chose to dress casually during the personal and group interviews with the young girls with whom I worked, because I wanted to minimize the appearance of formality. I was also aware of the possibility that my research participants could see me as a mother figure and that this could lead to the assumption that I would be listening to their narratives from the positions or characteristics that they ascribe to female figures in their community. I tried to minimize any inhibition in the narrative process by having group interviews to create a sense of "safety in numbers." I believed that a group setting would afford the participants the opportunity to observe my interaction with the others, and the results were apparent in the girls' ease with me and with each other. Although some of the participants were meeting each other for the first time, the connection they sensed in their stories helped create a safe space.

I was conscious of my position of power as interviewer from the beginning and set out to create some form of co-ownership of the study by changing the seating arrangements during the interviews. The personal interviews were conducted in a space that the school had provided, and I chose to sit at the side of the table rather than at the head in order to minimize the appearance of speaking from a place of authority. By allowing the participants to sit at the head of the table, I wanted to accord them some sense of ownership in the outcome of the interview process.

In addition, I positioned myself as learner during the interview process by sharing my personal reasons for the study. I informed them that I had daughters who were about the same age as they and that I wanted to better understand what the process of ethnic identity negotiation might mean to them. At my first meeting with the participants, I informed them of the paucity of research on West African immigrant girls, and by assuring them that they were the experts on their own experiences, I made them aware of the critical role they were playing in adding their voices, and subsequently the voices of other girls like them, to the literature. In doing this, I tried to establish a sense of obligation on the girls' part to a community of other girls who may never have the space to share their stories.

The notion of obligation to one's community, regardless of the temporal, historical, or geographical location of said community, is critical to Black, African, and endarkened feminist work (Steady, 1996; Dillard, 2006; hooks, 1994) and must inform the methodology that accompanies such work. This sense of community, wholeness, oneness, and obligation is the spirit of the work that takes into account the global community that is created out of African ascendant women's experiences with oppression. When I see myself and my experiences mirrored in my sisters' experiences halfway around the world and beyond, and right here in the voices of the new generation of transnational Black feminists, I begin to understand that the work I do is for all of us. This is an interconnectedness that removes me from the role of expert and thrusts us into a mutually rewarding and reciprocal teacher/learner relationship.

Finally, the methodology I have described is *a methodology that transcends research for research sake and pushes the work to a transformative level at which the researcher and the researched are changed in the experience.* The young woman who thanked me for allowing her to learn something about herself was also inspired to write about the study in her journal: "I can honestly say that it had me think about my future. With my parents' expectations, I wonder if I will have the same for [my] kids or not." The considerations of the role that African immigrant parents play and the ways their cultural expectations influence their children's ethnic identity choices caused the young woman to speculate whether she would behave in the same way when she became a parent. The fact that this young woman was placing her experiences in the larger context of the next generation speaks to the transformative power of an endarkened transnational methodology that begins to look at what the ethnic identification process will be like for third- and fourth-generation African immigrants.

The transformation I experienced in my work with the girls unfolded when I began to run into some of them very regularly after the study ended. I had never met the girls prior to the study, but in the year following its conclusion I crossed paths with them several times. I have met some of the parents of the girls and discussed some of the findings with them. One of the girls works part-time with my hairdresser, and whereas I may have run into her in this setting prior to the study, our relationship is now transformed by the time we spent together during the study. My transformation has culminated in the realization that the girls and I were connected even before the study took place. Our paths had probably crossed even then, but the difference is that we are no longer faceless. I now feel an obligation to the girls' well-being, and watching their progress through high school and beyond has enduring meaning for me. In the next chapter, I take up the notion of mentoring as research methodology to describe how mentoring guided the relationship between the participants and me during and after the study.

In contrast to the traditional research experience in which a researcher disconnects from the participants and the community when the study concludes, the young women and I realized that we were now obligated to each other. The study only served to connect us to a larger purpose that transcends the generational gap between us, a purpose that speaks to our interconnectedness, regardless of the specificity of our experiences.

Conclusion

At the beginning of this chapter I set out to show that the experiences of Black women in the diaspora with oppression, regardless of how the oppression is named, should serve as a source of connection rather than separation. Using data from a recent study on the experiences of African immigrant girls in the United States with racial subjugation and ethnic identification, and data from my own experiences with colonization, I suggested that an endarkened transnational feminist framework is an appropriate methodology for doing work with and for African ascendant women. I have attempted to redirect the conversations surrounding the naming of the feminist spirit beyond stances that might unwittingly be divisive and, instead, have advanced a position that more clearly encompasses the collectivity of African ascendant women's experiences with oppression in the diaspora. By embracing an endarkened transnational feminist epistemology, I have addressed the need for corresponding methodologies that transform the researcher, the research process, and the communities under study. The examples of appropriate methodologies I have given are by no means exhaustive, but act as a guidepost for those whose work might be viewed through the lenses of our interconnectedness as African ascendant women. As Dillard (2006) reminds us, methodologies for the work we do with African ascendant women must include a "commitment to a way of thinking and behaving that honors principles of inter-being and interconnectedness" (p. 77). Therefore, our ongoing conversation as endarkened transnational feminists is dynamic. As African ascendant women and as Africans, our experiences continue to reflect our movement around the world and the social, cultural, historical, and political spaces we occupy.

Note

1 This refers to the South African concept of Ubuntu (the belonging to a greater whole). It is a concept that links the individual's well-being to that of the community.

Chapter 3

The Diploma Belongs to Us

Mentoring African Immigrant Girls Through/For the Community

The mentoring experiences of Black women in the literature focus mostly on the mentoring relationships between Black female faculty and their graduate and professional school students, or peer mentorship among Black female graduate students (Patton, 2009; Henderson, Hunter, & Hildreth, 2010; Grant & Simmons, 2008; Holmes, Land, & Hinton-Hudson, 2007). The literature on Black women as mentors or mentees is replete with examples of the career trajectory of Black women who are mentored versus those who are not. Existing studies on the academic career experiences of the Black woman confirm two facts: (1) the literature on the Black female experience does not adequately capture the career needs, concerns, and achievements of the Black woman (Patton, 2009) and (2) even when these aspects of her experiences are covered, absent from the discourse are explanations for her ability to thrive in spite of the societal odds she faces (Patton, 2009). To fill this void, literature on the mentoring experiences of Black women provides examples of the roles that Black female mentors play in supporting other women as they climb the ladder in academia, corporations, and other walks of life.

Also present in the mentoring literature are instances of youth as recipients of the generosity of adult mentoring (Travis, 2010; Larose et al., 2011; Cayleff et al., 2011), as well as elementary-age students and youth benefitting from mentoring support for their emotional and mental disorders (Caldarella, Adams, Valentine, & Young, 2009; Jekielek, Moore, & Hair, 2002). There are also studies that have examined the impact of mentoring relationships on the development of at-risk adolescent girls (Quarles, Maldonado, & Lacey, 2005), as well as assessments of programs that explore the ways that relationships between mentors and their adolescent female mentees have been strengthened (Pryce, Silverton, & Sanchez, 2010).

The popular notion of mentorship in current literature typically describes the personal and professional development of the mentee as the sole purpose of a mentoring relationship (Patton, 2009; Fischler & Zachary, 2009; Henderson, Hunter, & Hildreth, 2010). Within this commonly held belief, the mentor is usually someone who has acquired knowledge and expertise and is positioned to impart these on a mentee or protégé. The resulting hierarchical relationship has been countered by liberating definitions of mentoring where the benefits are reciprocal, with both mentor and mentee benefiting from their interaction with one another (Fischler & Zachary, 2009).

There is not much in the mentoring literature that describes mentoring as research methodology or how the notion of a sustained relationship between the researcher and the participants, during and after the study, can be understood in the context of mentoring. That is the work that will be undertaken here.

In the last chapter I offered what I call transforming methodologies, which are meant to serve as guideposts for researchers who work with African ascendant women. One of the methodologies I described was *a methodology that transcends research for research's sake and pushes the work to a transformative level at which the researcher and the researched are changed in the experience.* In this chapter I will use the metaphor of hair braiding to illustrate how this particular methodology can help us understand mentoring as methodology.

Hair braiding is one of the more prevalent forms of body art in Africa (Babou, 2008). It can be an individual or communal form of expression. While types of body art might vary from one culture to another in form and meaning, the art of hair braiding is universally found in most African cultures (Babou, 2008). Therefore, as the presence of Black African immigrants has become increasingly noticeable in the major cities in which they settle, so has the proliferation of hair braiding centers. It is not uncommon to see large warehouses filled with women from various African countries for whom the primary income source is hair braiding. There are others who choose to conduct this business in their homes for the convenience as well as the cost saving that comes with not having to pay rent for space. Whether in their countries of origin or in the United States, hair braiding provides community-building opportunities among the braiders themselves and between them and their clients. It is not unusual to hear stories about events taking place in their home countries as well as gossip about their daily lives. These settings replicate communal scenes that they have left behind in their search for better lives (Babou, 2008).

So what does hair braiding have to do with a chapter on mentoring as a form of research methodology? Braids are used metaphorically to signify strength. Typically woven from three strands of hair, twine, cords, or other material, braids remind us of unity, community, and togetherness. In the Book of Ecclesiastes 4:12 (King James Version), King Solomon declares that "a threefold cord is not quickly broken." Braids have been used metaphorically in works such as Edwidge Danticat's *Krik? Krak!* (1996), in which she likens hair braiding to the act of writing. She compares the art of controlling unruly strands of hair as they are woven into a braid to the art of bringing unity to our words. Dixon (2005) also uses the metaphor of hair braiding to describe the methodological decisions she made concerning her research design. Using a step-by-step description of the hair braiding process, she explains how "the success of braiding is reliant on the sectioning and on the tensions between the strands in each braid and between braids" (p. 86). She likens this to the way she used strands from the fields of globalization and international higher education (IHE) in her researcher role as braider to show how she "constructed and communicated the repositioning of the international practice of institutions of higher education and produced contingent knowledge of globalisation as it is linked to IHE" (p. 87).

It is within these understandings of hair braiding as signifying complexity, strength, unity, and community that a study participant's mother and I engaged in conversations centering on immigration and identity as we worked on my daughter's braids one Saturday morning. We were engaged in an act that was symbolic of the ways mentoring can become the methodology that not only guides the work we do on behalf of the community, but also one that extends beyond the work. The traditional notion of mentoring was disrupted in the ways I set out to learn about my study participants as representative of the adolescent African immigrant experience, and I ended up seeing the African immigrant parent experience through their eyes.

When I embarked on the study of the experiences of West African immigrant adolescent girls in the United States with ethnic identity negotiations, I wanted to understand how home and school experiences shaped the ways they navigate their world as girls who are Black, African, African American, and American all at once and in various combinations of these identities. The goal of the study was that an understanding of the girls' stories might teach us about their educational and sociocultural needs and would allow educators to accommodate their needs in schools.

Utilizing a Black feminist theoretical framework (Collins, 1990), my goal was to provide a forum for these young women to share their otherwise silenced experiences and to enlighten us on how they are able to negotiate contextual identities with the fluidity that identification processes tend to demand of us. I had not met any of the participants prior to the study and had not given much thought to the possibility of running into them after the study was over. Contrary to my expectations, the researcher-participant relationship extended beyond the study, and I came to understand that my doctoral diploma served as more than a symbol of my personal and academic achievement. The mentor role that I have continued to play in the lives of the study participants has led to my consideration of the ways in which an endarkened feminist perspective (Dillard, 2000, 2006) might serve as a framework for examining the relationship that guided the study and that has continued between the participants and me. Dillard (2006) has examined what frameworks are available to us as African ascendant women for whom the big four paradigms (positivism, post-positivism, critical theory, and constructivism) may not necessarily be a fit. This includes a further examination of the ways that spirituality impacts the frameworks we choose for examining African ascendant women's lives. In response to the demands that these examinations make on our scholarship, Dillard has extended an endarkened feminist epistemology as a possible lens for viewing reality as it is perceived when based in Black feminist thought.

This chapter pushes the field to consider the notion of community embedded within the South African concept of Ubuntu (the belonging to a greater whole), as well as within endarkened feminist epistemology, and the implications for the researcher-as-mentor. Whereas traditional research practices have encouraged the concept of "research and run," in which the relationship with the participant concludes with researcher acquisition of the data, endarkened feminist framework encourages us to assume the metaphor of *research as a responsibility*, which makes demands on us as researchers to be obligated to the communities in/with which we work (Dillard, 2000, 2006). What follows is a brief explanation that demonstrates the use of an endarkened feminist framework as an effective lens for reviewing the researcher-participant relationship as it occurred within the context of mentoring.

Why an Endarkened Feminist Framework?

Endarkened feminist epistemology raises an important question for me as researcher: "How does spirituality impact the frameworks we choose for examining African ascendant women's lives?" The spiritual and epistemological stance of endarkened feminist epistemology is one in which the concept of individual well-being is predicated on the wholeness of the community (Dillard, 2006; Dillard & Okpalaoka, 2011). The spiritual concepts of communal wholeness and well-being found in the philosophy of Ubuntu sharply contradict the Western philosophy of individualism, a point that has been taken up by scholars such as Alexander (2005), Dillard (2006), hooks (2000), and Oyewumi (1997), to name a few. In the various roles I played during and after the research, I came to understand that my life and that of the participants became intertwined in ways that speak to the communal ownership of my diploma. In other words, I understood that if my degree did not lead to the betterment of my community, then it was only an acquisition that served my particular agenda.

Speaking of "the spiritual centering of teaching, research, and service from African and Black feminist frameworks," Dillard (2006, p. x) describes how her book *On Spiritual Strivings* seeks "to illuminate the transformative possibilities that lie in making more conscious connections to Africa in our work, and the process by which such connections can transform an academic life into one whose purpose is healing and service through teaching and research" (p. x). The key words for me in Dillard's description are "service" and "spirituality," both of which I believe are interchangeable, because to serve another is to acknowledge a human connection that transcends our physical sensibilities. What, then, do these two concepts mean in a study that is guided by an endarkened feminist framework?

Traditional research practices typically involve the researcher gaining access to a community, acquiring the required data, and leaving said community to begin the process of data analysis. In many instances, the relationship between the researcher and the participant ends with the study. In endarkened feminist epistemology, the metaphor of "research as responsibility" (Dillard, 2000, 2006) compels me to recognize that as an African ascendant researcher, I am a part of the community in which I work; therefore, "this necessitates a different relationship between me, as the researcher, and the researched..." (Dillard, 2006, p. 4). I maintained a connection with the participants beyond the study because our paths continued to cross in various contexts, and I was asked by them to serve in various mentor roles that confirmed that our lives were forever connected. Further defining endarkened feminist epistemology, Dillard (2006) directs our attention to the relationship between the researcher and the researched as one that is reciprocal. This contradicts traditional notions of the researcher/mentor as all-knowing and the one-sidedness that characterizes researcher/mentor and participant/mentee interactions. What, then, does research that is anchored in endarkened feminist praxis look like, and how can mentoring as methodology be understood within an endarkened feminist framework?

In Dillard & Okpalaoka (2011), we forward some considerations for engaging in endarkened transnational feminist research. One of these considerations in particular—*recognizing African community and landscapes*—points to the endarkened feminist researcher's commitment to "the sustained relationship" that research and dialogue require (p. 159). The researcher is encouraged to ask, "Are humility, sacrifice, and selflessness at the center of my desire to 'know'"? In other words, how can I, as researcher, be willing to practice a sustained commitment to the communities in which I work, knowing that the ultimate value of my work is the betterment of the communities to which I belong? I will now show how the mentoring relationship between the participants and me served as the methodology that guided the study as well as became the vehicle for sustained community and connectedness.

Mentoring as Method

Narrative research aided my investigation of how the girls in my study made meaning of their experiences of navigating the processes of ethnic identity construction. In keeping with Black and endarkened feminist frameworks that honor Black women's theorizing as having a legitimate place within mainstream educational research, participant narratives were gathered through personal and group interviews and participant journals. These three data collection methods were braided together to heighten the validity of the study (Guion, Diehl, & McDonald, 2002). The strength of the study lies in the comparison of data collection methods to see if similar conclusions were reached (Guion et al., 2002). Furthermore, since feminist writers such as Smith (1979) suggest that researchers begin with their own experiences, incorporating "their personal experiences and standpoints in their research by...explaining their personal connection to the project, or by using personal knowledge to help them in the research process" (Ellis & Bochner, 2003), I made my personal narrative a part of this study by helping the girls make a connection between their experiences with ethnic identity negotiations and mine as an African immigrant researcher, mother, daughter, and scholar. The study was also partly a result of my personal interest in the ethnic identity development of my teenage daughters and their peers who were also being raised in cultural and ethnic backgrounds similar to the study participants. By marshaling the ways in which my experiences and those of the participants were intertwined, my role as insider positioned me to demonstrate cultural sensitivity towards the girls' stories, and this, in turn, helped in my capture and interpretation of the data (Irvine, Roberts, & Bradbury-Jones, 2008).

The study revealed the influence that the sociocultural and national identities of the girls had on my role as mentor. Because my sociocultural and national identity was in line with that of the participants and allowed me to function in community with them, the notion of mentoring as method became apparent in the ways our cultural knowledge and experience set the tone for the interviews. The girls and I shared an understanding of family cultural expectations with regard to ethnic identity. Further, my position as a researcher who has also had to navigate cultural and identity boundaries gave me a deeper insight into the girls' experiences, especially on occasions when they struggled to articulate their thoughts. My lived experiences, made up of "beliefs, backgrounds, and feelings," positioned me not only as a co-constructor of knowledge with my participants (Hesse-Biber, 2006, p. 129), but also as mentor. As we engaged in a sort of "call and response," in which verbal and non-verbal cues marked the ways the girls and I responded to each other, I became a braider, and our shared experiences became the strands with which I worked to create an enduring relationship. The art of braiding demands time and patience. Each strand in the braid must be carefully isolated and intentionally intertwined with the others for a beautiful finish. I was able to identify and isolate the similarities and differences in the participants' experiences and mine and used these to create a trusting relationship predicated on a shared understanding of what it means to be of African ascent in the United States and the resultant ethnic and cultural identity implications. Leveraging my own ethnic and cultural identity negotiations as an immigrant who is at the same time a U.S. native, scholar, mother, employee, and educator who has had to explain my presence in the many spheres I occupy, I was able to support the participants in what I understood to be their individual journeys in ethnic and cultural self-awareness.

The study revealed that the participants and their families were engaged in the negotiation of sociocultural practices and expectations that were sometimes tension-filled. My knowledge of and engagement in similar negotiations enhanced my understanding of the interplay between the girls and their parents. They also helped me understand that as noble as my efforts were at expecting my children to maintain strong ties to their Nigerian heritage for the sake of cultural preservation, the personal agency and the importance the participants attributed to their sense of choice in their ethnic identity construction was a lesson for me as well as for their parents. One particular example of an interaction with the participants caused me to reflect on my role as an African immigrant parent and gave me insight into the ways I was complicit in maintaining patriarchal standards. The contrast between ethnic and dominant cultural norms usually manifests in beliefs about gender equality, dating, and marriage (Dasgupta, 1998). For example, some Asian Indian parents' choice of marriage partners for their female children is usually preceded by restrictions on dating (Das & Kemp, 1997). This is contrasted by the Western practice of permitting adolescents to date and eventually pick their marriage partners. Studies such as Lee's (2005) indicate that patriarchal practices are transported to the United States by immigrants and result in tension between the different generations in the home. Some of this tension arises from the differences in the ways male and female children are raised in that female children are expected to maintain their family culture and tradition (Stritikus & Nguyen, 2007). Findings from my study suggested that African immigrant families still held traditional beliefs about dating and marriage and were transplanting traditional beliefs about gender roles to the United States. These roles include cooking, keeping the home, and other activities that are gender-specific. The girls in the study confirmed that they are expected to fulfill certain gender roles at home. Describing why they were expected to know how to cook and clean the home, some of the girls responded, "preparation for marriage." One girl, whom I will call Abena, lamented:

> But the number one thing is you always gotta stay in the kitchen. That gets on my nerves sometimes. Even when I'm doing my homework, [my mother says] "Come and watch when I'm cooking." (focus group, February 28, 2008)

When I probed a little further, her response revealed that she was expected to fulfill certain roles in the house so that it would appear that her parents were doing their job as parents, and that people would know that she's "trained at home." As I have described elsewhere in this book, in many African societies, the way a girl is "trained" reflects her parents' child-rearing skills, especially her mother's. A mother wants to ensure that her daughters learn all the female responsibilities such as cooking, cleaning, and caring for the home. In addition to proving to the community that the girl has been raised well, it also proves to her future spouse and in-laws that her mother played her part in raising her well—hence the emphasis on girls being in the kitchen with their mothers. I have wrestled with this issue myself as a mother of two teenage daughters. I understand the importance of their learning to care for their homes, but I struggle with passing down traditions that will maintain current gender expectations that only females should do housework. This may apply in African societies that are still mostly patriarchal, but I understand that they are being raised in a completely different context, one in which every member of the household is expected to contribute to the upkeep of the home. Hearing the girls discuss the tension between themselves and their parents caused me to reflect on the reasons why my daughters and I were engaged in similar tension-filled dialogue. I realized that I, too, wanted to appear as though I had raised them well—to be "good" wives someday. I was engaged in passing down traditional gender practices to girls whose future family dynamics were likely to be different from mine.

I went into the study to learn about the girls, but I ended up learning about the limitations of my influence on my children's ethnic identity choices. The new awareness I have described speaks to the *reciprocity* of our mentoring relationship and was captured by one of the participants, who stated: "though you learn[ed] something from us girls, us girls can also say we learned something about ourselves" (journal entry, March 10, 2008). Her journal entry confirmed that she recognized my position as learner in the research relationship. In contrast to traditional, one-sided mentoring relationships, what occurred between the participants and me was reciprocated, "as every person [was] both teacher and taught, changing as we know the other and the other knows us" (Dillard & Okpalaoka, p. 158). I *heard* the girls' stories through my researcher role, but it was as an immigrant parent that I came to understand that my work in helping them to articulate their awareness of their ethnic identity negotiations was mutually rewarding in the awareness I gained of the contextual identities that they and others like them were able to wield.

Mentoring requires not only patience but *deliberate* and *intentional* listening as well. I recognized the humanity of these girls and understood that they were not merely data sources. They carried within them stories they had been waiting for time and opportunity to tell. Caught between parental expectations of conformity to the family ethnic identity and practices and the ethnic identity expectations that society thrust upon them, these girls needed a space to articulate what it means to be Black adolescent girls being raised in African immigrant homes in the United States. I argue that the girls' feeling of being heard contributed to the trust that developed between us and led to the invitation they extended to me to participate in their lives beyond the study.

Beyond the Study: Shifting Researcher Identity

> *I really enjoyed the interview, and it is the first time I feel safe to open up to someone.* (Ekene, personal interview, March 2008)

At the beginning of the study, I was aware that my research participants might view me as a "mother figure" and that this could lead to their perception of me as a judgmental listener. I was concerned that this would hinder the narrative process. My choice of the focus group as an additional method of data collection was to create a sense of "safety in numbers" for the girls. I also believed that it would afford the participants the opportunity to experience my interaction with the others. I saw the result in the girls' apparent relaxation with me and each other, which was later confirmed by a journal entry made by one of the participants: "I really enjoyed the interview, and it is the first time I feel safe to open up to someone." And to quote another girl, "Thank you for letting me take part in your study."

The mentor role earned me invitations to several of the participants' high school graduation parties—invitations that I honored, to the girls' delight. I began to run into one of them at my daughter's hairdresser, where the young woman regularly helped out. Soon she was regularly assisting the hairdresser with braiding my daughter's hair. This was one of the contexts in which my identity as researcher shifted and where I assumed the continued role of mentor as the girl and I became members of a community different from the one that first brought us together. In the summer before her senior year, she asked me to review her college application essay. It was to me she turned when she questioned her guidance counselor's advice to apply to the regional campus of a major university rather than the main campus, because the counselor believed the young girl stood a better chance of being accepted there. I advised her at that time to apply to the main campus and allow the application reviewers to make that decision.

In the years since, I have continued to cross paths with the girls, even as one of them changed schools and became friends with my daughter, while the others connected with another daughter through social media. This connection gives me a sense of responsibility toward these young women's well-being and an obligation to our larger community. I see the way that their stories and their families' stories resonate with mine and my family's. *I am because we are.*

An endarkened feminist view of the connections I made with the participants during and after the study directs our attention to "the powerful and omnipresent role of community" (Dillard &

Okpalaoka, 2011, p. 159) by placing community at the center of my work with the girls. The stories that the girls had shared with me were confirmed as well within the context of community, as I will explain in the next section. I began this chapter with the metaphor of braiding, and I will end by describing a full-circle experience that illustrates how the endarkened feminist notion of honoring the communities in which we work turned a mundane task such as hair braiding into a significant moment, thereby supporting Collins's (2003) foregrounding of Black women's use of narratives and daily conversations as locations for articulating core themes of Black feminist consciousness.

The Gift That Keeps on Giving:
When Data Analysis Comes Full Circle

> ...if we understand that what we are sharing is more than data, that we are giving our stories as gifts to one another, then we will understand that when anyone offers us a glimpse into their pain, dreams, hopes, whatever...we should receive it with open hands, gently and honorably, and treasure it for the privilege it is. (Okpalaoka & Dillard, 2011)

Russell, in the pioneering Black feminist volume *But Some of Us Are Brave* (1982), describes storytelling as "the oldest form of building historical consciousness in community" (p. 198). Further describing storytelling as "the deliberate accumulation of a people's collective memory" (p. 198), Russell illustrates the value that storytelling can bring to the context in which I recently found myself. It was a beautiful autumn Saturday morning when I arrived at my hairdresser's to have my daughter's braids taken out. Upon arrival, I recognized the mother of one of the girls whom I had interviewed 4 years earlier. Unbeknownst to me, the hairdresser had recruited the mother to help take out my daughter's braids. I later learned that this was not unusual and was the hairdresser's way of helping this mother, who had not worked for over 10 years because she is on dialysis. I had brought some work to do to pass the time, but learned very quickly that this was going to be one of those moments that arrives unheralded, and I was not going to let my best-laid plans interfere with one of those "daily conversations" that Collins (2000) describes as sites for articulating core themes of Black feminist consciousness. We began by discussing how her daughter, a college sophomore, was doing.

Our conversation soon turned to what it means to raise African immigrant children in the United States, and my companion for the afternoon shared her efforts at maintaining ties to her Ghanaian roots by ensuring that she speaks to her children in their native language and by making Ghanaian meals. She described how she had quickly corrected her daughter upon hearing her declare that she was American by reminding her of her African roots. We soon went on to other matters as she shared her health problems with kidney failure and dialysis. By this time, I had joined her in taking out my daughter's braids. This woman was sharing her life story with me, and I wanted to honor her gift by settling into the moment. Even though I was going to pay her full price for taking out my daughter's braids, I knew that the act of taking out braids together as she shared her story was symbolic. As Collins (2000) explains, I was "draw[ing] on the tradition of using everyday actions and experiences" as theoretical work (p. 33). I was no longer a client, but a collaborator in the task before us—a task that included "spiritual solidarity... [in our] becom[ing] fully life-affirming" (hooks, 1993). We were engaged in dialogue that is central to Black feminist (Collins, 2000) and endarkened feminist lives.

Two hours passed, and we were soon done. We had shared so much that reminded me of how interconnected our experiences as African ascendant people are, regardless of our location in the diaspora (Dillard & Okpalaoka, 2011; Okpalaoka & Dillard, 2012). As she told her story, she corroborated the stories her daughter had shared during the study. I drove home humbled by what had just occurred. This woman had trusted me with her story because of my relationship with her daughter. She, too, recognized that our relationship was no longer that of researcher-participant; rather, we were now in community with one another based on our shared cultural knowledge and experiences. What we were engaged in was larger than the two of us. We were engaged in an actual hairbraiding ritual that was reflected in the coming together of our experiences. As our hands worked on the braids in my daughter's hair, our corroborated stories worked together to secure a space in which the researcher and the researched, the knower and the known, were stronger in recognizing that each was not alone. In that moment I was, all at once, the mother before me as well as her daughter with whom I had worked. As Dillard (2012) proclaimed, "...I am not my sister or brother's keeper, I am my sister or brother" (p. 105). *I am because we are.*

What, then, does this mean for scholars who work in the very communities they share with their participants? How might scholars who engage in research with Black girls and their navigation of contextual identities consider their commitment to relationships that extend beyond the study? Dillard (2006) asserts that too often as researchers we expect to remain the same in the work we do, thinking that our task entails only theorizing our findings. Instead, she says that "spiritually, researchers can also be transformed by the work that we do. And if we are not spiritually transformed by the work that we do, we remain at the same point, engaging the same principles—the 'way' that we began" (p. 86). Dillard goes on to describe why our methodological choices have to be spiritual in nature as a response to the reciprocal relationship that develops between researcher and participant as they become teacher or student in each other's lives. Based on these realizations, I propose the following.

First, employing mentoring as a research method will determine the type of questions we ask as researchers and what we do with the responses we get. When the participants described the active role they played in their ethnic identity construction in spite of family sociocultural expectations, I heard their stories as both researcher and parent of children similarly engaged in those processes of identity negotiation. The insights I received into the everyday interactions I have with my children were valuable. I entered the study to learn about the girls and came out learning about myself. Even in their participant roles, the girls' stories were "specialized bodies of knowledge...legitimate and powerful" (Dillard, 2006, p. 6).

Second, although the participants and I physically left the study site at the study's conclusion, the researcher-participant role was reconfigured in my continuing role as mentor. Choosing mentoring as a research method means rejecting the detached position of the traditional researcher and engaging the community in which we work both during and after the study.

Third, it is important to acknowledge the ways that a shared sociocultural and national identity with study participants can privilege the researcher's understanding of nuances that may be particular to the community. I was able to function in community with the girls because our cultural knowledge and understandings set the tone for our interactions during the study.

Finally, the notion of mentoring as method challenges us to seek a "higher moral responsibility" (Dillard, 2006) that transcends our pursuit of career advancement and that causes us to reach back and bring others alongside us. The product of a research study is only beneficial to the community to the extent that the researcher assumes a posture that is caring, engaging, and committed to the community. The researcher and her research are only as successful as the community is. Only then can the researcher and the community lay claim to the wholeness and belongingness to a greater whole that is inherent in Ubuntu: *I am because we are.*

Chapter 4

Wisdom Lost and Regained

My Life as a Generational Bridge Across Three Migrations

When we think of bridges, we imagine structures made of steel, wood, or other durable material and spanning disconnected land masses separated by water or other impassable terrain. Bridges can be arched or straight, rustic or sophisticated. But they are all built to stand the test of time and the elements. The word "bridge" can be used metaphorically to denote a connection between people, time, and place. Anzaldúa, in her preface to *This Bridge We Call Home: Radical Visions for Transformation* (Anzaldúa & Keating, 2002), speaks of bridges as "passageways, conduits, and connectors that connote transitioning, crossing borders, and changing perspectives. Bridges span liminal (threshold) spaces between worlds..." (p. 1). Anzaldúa goes on to discuss the transformation that occurs in these liminal, in-between places where we are never at home. We are constantly battling feelings of displacement and discomfort even when we come to call such places home. In *Borderlands/La Frontera: The New Mestiza*, Anzaldúa also refers to the positionality of being in a "state of transition" (p. 100) while "simultaneously straddling...two or more cultures" (p. 102).

Less overtly, Collins (2000) appropriates the bridge metaphor by linking African American women's experiences with oppression with that of women of African descent globally. In the second edition of her *Black Feminist Thought*, she takes up African American women's positionality within a global Black feminism to show how we cannot talk about social justice struggles for Black women in the United States without looking beyond our borders to examine how our sisters are faring in other parts of the world. Arguing for a transnational gaze on the shared legacy that women of African descent have with systems of oppression, Collins (2000) leads us to understand the ways that racial oppressions, organized through slavery, colonialism, and imperialism, move across national borders made porous by modern technology. Even when the particularities of oppression differ, the goal is the same—to keep Black women subjugated (Collins, 2000; Ogundipe-Leslie, 1994).

The oppression of African ascendant people has been demonstrated in historical and contemporary contexts, and

> the key difference lies in the organization of particular oppressions. Said another way, though contexts of domination might be similar across the globe (in that there is some combination of interlocking systems of oppression), the differences arise in the ways these particular oppressions manifest and the historical roots of said oppressions. The type of clothing that oppression is dressed in (that is, apartheid, colonialism, imperialism, enslavement) may vary. However they are all systems of oppression, intersecting in various combinations and contexts. (Dillard & Okpalaoka, 2011, p. 149)

Acknowledging the complexities of Black and endarkened feminisms and epistemologies that link the continent of Africa and the African diaspora, Dillard and Okpalaoka (2011) suggest that we embrace the spiritual and the sacred, inherent in endarkened feminist epistemology, as alternative but legitimate responses to the connectedness of Black women's experiences with domination. An endarkened feminist approach to research is one "that honors the wisdom, spirituality and critical interventions of transnational Black woman's ways of knowing and being in research, with the sacred serving as a way to describe the doing of it, the way that we approach the work" (p. 148). African feminist Oyeronke Oyewumi (1997), in demonstrating the ways that imperialism and Western domination have spanned geographical and temporal boundaries, suggests that the Atlantic slave trade and European colonization of Africa "were logically one process unfolding over many centuries" (p. xi).

What Anzaldúa, Oyewumi, Collins, and others are suggesting, then, is that whether in the United States or the diaspora, African ascendant peoples' experiences are bridged by their past, present, and continuous movements across national borders, even as we continue to negotiate cultural memory, history, and identity in the in-between spaces we find ourselves.

In this chapter I tell a personal story that I hope helps to address the dearth of scholarship on the Black African immigrant experience across time, what might have been lost or gained in the movements of African ascendant peoples, as well as the layered identities we have assumed in the diaspora. I will show how generational feminist knowledge and wisdom carried within the migrations of African people, as well as in the voices of our feminist grandmothers, are always mediated by cultural memory to help us (re)member who we are/were.

In describing how this knowledge and wisdom has been lost and gained in the migrations of African people back and forth across the waters, I will share the migratory experiences of three generations of my family and show how we have come to straddle histories, cultures, and identities in the liminal spaces which Anzaldúa describes. Using the metaphor of a bridge, I will demonstrate how my life experiences and positionality as daughter and mother mediate generational relationships within my family as we negotiate all the places we call home. Several questions will be raised here: (1) How do our lives represent the ways that African ascendant people have come to be across language, culture, and space? (2) How do I serve as a bridge between and across generations of my family who, in various ways, are in constant movement across the waters?

The Beginnings

In 1964, a young college graduate and his bride left the Nigerian shores for the United States. He was one of the young men and women who were privileged to pursue graduate work outside the country, some sponsored by families who could afford to pay for their education, others the recipients of scholarships from foreign philanthropic organizations. The young couple arrived filled with the hopes and dreams of getting an education and returning home to serve their newly independent nation. I was born in the spring of the following year as they quickly settled into their new lives and school. As with many newcomers, their first cultural contact with the United States was through the education system (Arthur, 2000). While my father completed graduate work at Michigan State University, my mother attended secretarial school. All around them were the signs of the times—the turmoil and unrest stemming from the Civil Rights Movement—and they did not escape the volatility of the racial tensions of the time.

Black African immigrants, although familiar with inter-ethnic group dynamics in their home countries, are unaccustomed to the complicated nature of race relations that exists in the United States. It is here that they are confronted, for the first time, with a pan-national identity (African) as opposed to a national identity (Nigerian). Racist events and encounters might cause the African immigrant to see him or herself primarily as a racial being in the United States, in contrast to any pre-migratory ethnic identification that he or she possessed. Consequently, African immigrants who have been the majority in their home countries find themselves to be minorities in the United States, resulting in a heightened awareness of racism and the significance of belonging to a marginalized group (Cross, 1995).

As early as 1938, Reid made reference to the dual adjustment of the Negro immigrant, which requires a closer look at his experiences with intra- and inter-racial relations in the United States.

> Every foreign-born Negro must readjust the concepts of "class" and "caste" to which he has been accustomed in terms of the United States' racial pattern. He has left a setting where he was one of the subjugated majority, or a hybrid status thereof, to come to one where he is one of the underprivileged racial minority.... (Reid, 1938, p. 412)

While the Civil Rights Era unfolded in the United States, African nations were engaged in their own struggles for independence from colonial rule. So, even though African immigrants of the 1960s like my parents were leaving their own struggles with independence and ethnic turmoil behind, they soon discovered that struggle marked the Black experience everywhere (Collins, 2000; Nnaemeka, 1998; Dillard & Okpalaoka, 2011).

My family's first sojourn in the United States was interrupted by the onset of the Nigerian Civil War, and we had to return home to the palpable inter-ethnic distrust and fear that marked the fate of a nation on the threshold of war. It might appear odd that we would head home to a country at war rather than remain in the United States, but home was calling, and my mother, the only surviving child of her father (she lost her mother at a very young age and her only brother later), could not stay away. Although she was thousands of miles away, she never felt at home. She had her memories of the naysayers who had balked at the idea that my grandfather had allowed his only child and daughter to travel to the White man's land. The community had expected her to abide by tradition and remain in her father's house to bear sons who would carry on the family name.

Although applicable to a lesser degree today, in the patriarchal Igbo culture, the birth of a male child is heralded with much fanfare, because it is the male child who carries on the family lineage by keeping the family name. Hence, a name like Ositadinma (which in Igbo means "today is the beginning of good things") is given to a much-awaited male child to mark the beginning of good things in the family, further implying that there is not much to celebrate in the birth of a female child. This is partly because the female child will traditionally adopt her husband's name when they get married, thereby disrupting the possibility of carrying on the family name.

Azuah (2005) also describes the practice among the Igbos of Nigeria of a widow without a male offspring assuming the role of a "female husband" by "marrying" a wife. The wife takes in male lovers with whom she bears children who eventually belong to the female husband and carry on her husband's name. This practice also exists in families with all-female children who, in order to preserve the family lineage, require one of the daughters to stay home and sacrifice the prospect of marriage. The daughter assumes the role of a son and takes on the responsibility of bearing male children. By allowing my mother not only to get married but also to travel very far from home, my grandfather showed that he was ahead of his time. So this was the cultural context in which my mother's departure from Nigeria occurred, and it was the reason for her insistence on returning home in time of war. I have included this particular story to illustrate the complex nature of culture and tradition in the lives of African ascendant people and how these are transported as we move around and settle in other places, especially since Ogundipe-Leslie (1994) claims that "African women...wish to retain certain features of their traditions; those which are positive for women" (p. 13).

One might then ask why a very young republic was already at war barely 7 years after its independence and why, after more than a century of British rule and an opportunity to be self-governing, things fell apart so rapidly. In his latest book, *There Was a Country*, Chinua Achebe (2012) traces the assault of Western imperialism from the so-called "discovery" of Africa to the transatlantic slave trade and the scramble for Africa at the 1885 Berlin Conference, which resulted in disrupted geographical boundaries. Britain's portion of the partitioned continent was the area that is today known as Nigeria. The advent of British rule in Nigeria interfered with existing formal and informal political and governance structures. Taking advantage of already-existing monarchies, the British successfully implemented the practice of indirect rule by simply switching the peoples' allegiance from their former rulers to the British. The Igbos did not have a monarchy, and direct rule was the only option for governance. Facing a shortage of British administrators and needing additional personnel to assist in the governing process, the colonial government created the system of warrant chiefs among the Igbos (Achebe, 2012; Eluwa, Ukagwu, Nwachukwu, & Nwaubani, 1988). These men were mostly figureheads who did not have much direct input in governance.

The disruption of geographical boundaries and traditional political institutions led to internal problems that were only compounded when British rule ended and eventually resulted in what Achebe (2012) called "a tension-prone modern state(s)" (p. 1). When the Northern and Southern protectorates of Nigeria were amalgamated, no one could have predicted the effect on civil, political, and ethnic relations that endures today. The optimism that marked the independence of Nigeria was soon interrupted by political unrest that pitted the Igbos and the rest of the country against one another. Eluwa and colleagues (1988) argue that when Nigerian leaders, in their zeal for independence, made compromises that did not factor in the looming ethnic divisiveness, issues of unequal opportunity and fair sharing of the nation's economic wealth, the stage was set for civil war. This was the situation to which we returned in 1966, and for the next 4 years we learned to live in less than ideal circumstances with the ever-present fear of being bombed by enemy planes.

I still have memories of my family and our neighbors running for cover in underground shelters when we heard the sound of fighter planes overhead. The young couple, who had left Nigeria only a few years back, now had to adjust to frequent enemy raids and long separations from each other while my father left home to find work. Meanwhile, my mother found creative ways to protect our family from starvation and malnutrition by discovering plants that were previously viewed as inedible. There was, though, one constant in all of the uncertainty of war: my parents' determination that I continue my education whether in one-room schoolhouses or at home. And as soon as I could reach my hand over my head and touch the opposite ear,[1] I was officially ready for first grade. The importance that my family placed on my getting an education in the midst of the uncertainty of war has been significant in my educational journey and has been transferred to succeeding generations.

Coming of Age

By the time I came of age in the early 1970s, the residual signs of colonialism were still apparent in the presence of Western expatriates in our schools and government institutions. At the time, I was enrolled in an international primary school along with expatriate children. When I think of the ways that my early memories make a demand on the present work that I do concerning race, identity, and the marginalization of African ascendant peoples, I reflect on the ways my college-educated father and his work positioned us to live in neighborhoods that held reminders of colonial rule and the social hierarchy of earlier decades. I remember growing up in a neighborhood where our home was surrounded on all sides by the homes of Western expatriates and the boys' quarters in which their Nigerian male and female help lived. Because Saturdays and Sundays were the only days I did not have to leave home early for school, I would awaken to the aroma of food coming from one of the neighboring homes. I wanted to know what the people on the other side of the fence ate. There was no interaction with our neighbors except when we scaled the fence to pick whatever fruit was in season, only to be chased away. I got an opportunity to satisfy my curiosity the day I was taken over to one of the boys' quarters to have my hair braided, and I smelled the same aroma that I now associated with that part of the world. In my childhood innocence, I asked the man cooking over the stove what the aroma was. It was from the pancakes he was making for the White priests who lived in the home. I got to taste the pancakes and found that they did not smell or taste like the ones I was used to. I was not particularly aware and did not make the connection to the ways that the living arrangements of the man and his family mirrored that of the help who worked in our home and the homes of other Nigerian civil servants who were gradually filling positions vacated by the British. This was one of the legacies of the hierarchical living arrangements instituted by the British, which separated the help from those they served (Amole, 1992).

I now question the concept of a boys' quarter and the derogatory connotations of the word "boy," which reveals the ways in which we were all implicated in the maintenance of a class structure that separated living quarters, with the help living behind the main house. It also holds reminders of the days when slaves lived in small shacks behind the main house. Young (1999) describes how those humble slave dwellings were designed to remind their occupants of their low station, as compared to the more stately dwellings of the slaveowners and overseers. Ellis and Ginsburg (2010) also address the slaveowners' deliberate placement of slave cabins to reinforce the slaves' inferior station. In juxtaposing the living arrangements of present-day housegirls and houseboys with what existed during the slave era, I am only illustrating the ways that the oppressor, at different times in history and in different contexts, maintains power by keeping the oppressed in their place. I am also demonstrating the ways that the oppressed tend to mirror oppressors' behaviors themselves. Freire's (2000) account of the oppressed/oppressor contradiction explains the irony in events that followed—when those who fought for independence from colonialism soon adopted the ways of the colonialists. In *The Beautyful Ones Are Not Yet Born* (1968), Ayi Kwei Armah describes the events that followed the overthrow of Ghana's first post-colonial president, Kwame Nkrumah. The so-called socialist leaders, in their desire to acquire wealth, only mimicked the capitalist colonial regime from which they had just won independence. Similarly, Chinua Achebe, in *A Man of the People* (1966), also illustrates how the minister of culture, Mr. Nanga, uses his political influence for self-aggrandizement rather than for the uplifting of his people. This was the political climate in which I came of age and which set the stage for the steady current of emigration that was to follow.

I Am My Sister's Keeper

As soon as I was old enough to understand, I learned that I was an American citizen. I did not attach any meaning or importance to this fact, for there was no immediate need for me to return to or identify with the United States. Most of what I learned about the United States and the rest of the world was from school textbooks. The rest I learned by being an avid reader of fiction and nonfiction. (Television did not become a household staple until much later.) In school texts, I learned of the transatlantic slave trade, which robbed the African continent of millions of lives and decimated a major human power base. And in children's books such as *The Bobbsey Twins*, I was introduced to Sam and Dinah, the Black live-in servants who spoke in thick dialect: *"Well, I declar' to gracious!... If yo' chillum ain't gone an' mussed up de floah ag'in!"* (Hope, 2005, p. 7). Therefore, like many immigrants, some of my pre-migratory knowledge of African Americans was shaped by these stereotypes, which indicated that their circumstances were defined primarily by their slavery or maid status. Much later, television would also wreak its own havoc through the images it consistently streamed about African Americans' lives.

An understated narrative was the historical and spiritual connection I shared with my brothers and sisters who were forcibly removed and taken to distant shores. The narratives diminished the association between the Africans who were sold into slavery and those left behind. Slavery was their story, their experience, separate from mine; overlooked was the fact that my sister's story, on one side of the Atlantic, was tied to my own story, on the other side of the ocean. Collins (2000) rightly asserts that confronting social injustices as African ascendant people necessitates our coming to terms with our "particular group history" in order to build an effective coalition (p. 247). She cautions that even though Nigerian and U.S. Black women have been victimized, our coalition building must extend beyond our shared victimization to acknowledge that the sources and forms of victimization are not the same.

With this in mind, I began to research how connected the transatlantic slave trade was to places I knew as home. My mother is from a part of Eastern Nigeria settled by the Ndoki people. The villages that make up Ndoki are Akwete, Ohambele, Azumini, Obunko, Ohanku (my mother's village), Obehie, and Umuagbayi (Chuku, 2005). The Azumini Blue River, which runs through Ndoki, historically served as a conduit for the Portuguese, Spanish, and English slave traders' infiltration into the hinterlands and has been recognized as the last stop for slaves in Igbo land. Johnston A.K. Njoku, of Western Kentucky University, has conducted extensive fieldwork in Nigeria under the Freedom to Freedom Trail Project to heighten awareness of the transatlantic slave trade in Nigeria. Referring to Njoku's work, Cummings (2003) explains that although over 50% of African slaves came from a region of West Africa named the Slave Coast (which included

Nigeria) by the European slave traders, the more commonly known points of the slave journey are the Grain Coast (mostly Senegal and Gambia), the Ivory Coast (now Côte d'Ivoire), and the Gold Coast (now Ghana). Focusing on the significant role of the town of Arochukwu (in Eastern Nigeria) as a slave-trading and processing center, Njoku traces the slaves' journeys from Arochukwu to the then-interior slave markets and slaveholding quarters in Ututu, Bende, and Azumini before the journey onward to the coastal towns of Bonny and Calabar to the Atlantic Ocean.

Njoku (2003) describes the purpose of the Freedom to Freedom Trail Project as a journey of healing, reconciliation, and freedom from North America back to the former Slave Coast, a journey to which Dillard (2006) alludes in her poem "I Am Here in the World" from *On Spiritual Strivings: Transforming an African American Woman's Academic Life*:

> I have always been here in Africa,
> but now I know
> from having walked Her earth
> over and over again,
> I know
> way deep down inside my bones,
> the place where the strength
> of the African American comes
> and
> I can see
> what I am and
> who I am
> and I can live in that space
> for the rest of my life.... (p. 50)

Describing a journey back to Ghana with her older sister, mother, and two aunts, Dillard (2006) also explains the necessity of the journey: "to help them find *home* in Ghana" and "to observe and participate in their experiences of 'homecoming' to Africa, to occupy together a space that was both transformative and healing to us all, as persons of African ascent" (p. 55). Like Dillard, hooks (2000) argues that when we seek well-being within a healing context, our focus should not be on remaining victims of our circumstances or blaming others. Dillard and hooks take up a very pertinent subject that directs our gaze to the enduring ties between continental Africans and African Americans in the United

States and the ways that we can work toward healing and reconciliation.

Today there are more recent African immigrants in the United States than there have been since the Immigration Act was passed in 1965. Many of us have our feet firmly planted in Africa and the United States, just as many of our African American kinfolks do. It is important to note that our movements back and forth across the waters call up questions of identity that are more pertinent today than they ever have been. What do we lose—or what have we lost—in these journeys, and what have we gained?

The next section takes up issues concerning the wisdom that is lost and regained in the continuous movement across the waters in which my family and I are engaged, and how my life serves as a bridge across three generations. I will show how my position as daughter and mother, as the bridge generation between my parents and my children, metaphorically represents a link between the old and the new, the lost and the regained. This position has afforded me the lenses through which I observe inter- and intra-generational relations as they occur around our bridging of the gaps in history, tradition, and cultural memory between what once was and what is.

My Life as a Bridge

I returned to the United States in 1991 after learning that my U.S. citizenship granted me full rights not only to enter the country at will but also to live here. I had been married for barely 2 years at this time and immediately began the process of emigrating with my husband and daughter. We were not alone in our migratory plans. African immigrants surveyed by Arthur (2000) cite four main reasons for coming to the United States. They immigrate for postsecondary education, to reunite with family members, to take advantage of economic opportunities, and to escape from political terror and instability. During this decade, Nigeria, like many African countries, was in the midst of political and economic decline and imposed austerity measures on its citizens. Economic underdevelopment and unstable government, which were attributable to colonial and post-colonial rule as well as failed transfer of power, accounted for and continue to account for the migration of citizens of many African nations (Onimode, 1982; Adeyanju & Oriola, 2011; Takougang, 1995). Beginning in the mid-1980s, there was an exodus of nurses, doctors, and other healthcare professionals to the United States, the U.K, and the Middle East to help ease the shortage of healthcare workers in these nations. By the mid-1990s, other professionals, including college professors like my father, joined the migration bandwagon. The Diversity Lottery Visa Program, instituted in 1995, enabled my parents to re-enter the United States 5 years after I did—this time not as students but as professionals seeking to begin new lives in a more economically stable environment. The Diversity Lottery Visa Program has been responsible for bringing in a population of immigrants much older than usual. This collective of older immigrants includes a significant number of people who were close to retirement age in their home country but who were forced to seek greener pastures in the face of rapidly declining economies and unstable governments. The stories of disruption in the lives they knew and the creation of new lives at a time when they should have been settling into retirement are stories of regret, resignation, and the realization that they now have to be "willing to get rid of the life [they'd] planned so as to have the life that is waiting for [them]" (Campbell; cited in Osbon, 1991).

In the years that followed, my parents lived with my family and, when they were able, lived close by. This is not an unusual progression in the living arrangements of immigrant families. Landale, Thomas, and Van Hook (2011) reiterate the importance of such set-ups in shaping the integration of immigrant families into U.S. society. The authors specify the presence of grandparents as one of the key features of these living arrangements. It is therefore not uncommon for tensions to arise from differences in child-rearing practices, as well as the complex processes of maintaining customs and traditions as a means of preserving ties to the home country. The literature on immigrant ethnic identity development is replete with studies that have examined the critical role of families in the ethnic identity formation of immigrant adolescents (Umana-Taylor, Bhanot, & Shin, 2006; Umana-Taylor & Fine, 2004; Okpalaoka, 2009a). These studies also indicate that patriarchal practices are transported to the United States by immigrants and result in tensions between the different generations in the home (Lee, 2005). Some of this tension arises from the differences in the ways male and female children are raised (Dion & Dion, 1996). Stritikus and Nguyen (2007) and Dion and Dion

(2004) confirm that female children, unlike their male counterparts, are expected to maintain their family culture and tradition.

My parents represent a generation of immigrants who have spent more time in their homeland than in the United States and can be described as repositories of our customs and traditions. I, on the other hand, am representative of first-generation Nigerian immigrants who are caught between the more rigid expectations of cultural maintenance of my parents and my second-generation children, who are continuously redefining what their Nigerian backgrounds mean to their ethnic identification process. My identity is further complicated by the fact that I am an American by birth as well as a Nigerian who was raised in Nigeria for most of my childhood and early adult years. I have lived an equal number of years in Nigeria and the United States. Thus I am able to navigate both histories and cultures efficiently and in a manner that neither my parents nor my children can. In spite of our generational differences, we are all engaged in our own ways with remembering culture and history in ways that are spiritually transforming (Dillard & Okpalaoka, 2011).

We have been privileged with opportunities for addressing questions about the ethnic identity development of our children, who are caught up in the demands that old and new customs and traditions make of their identity formation. I will share a brief scenario that captures the ways I constantly bridge the divide between the old (represented by my parents) and the new (represented by my children).

I am in the midst of the daily ritual of making dinner when I call my 17-year-old daughter (at that time) to the kitchen to admonish her for not being in the kitchen with me while I am cooking. I was raised to believe that girls should be in the kitchen with their mothers, since that is the only way they can learn the art of cooking. My mother, who is visiting for a while, chimes in with her concern that my daughter does not show any interest in learning. I can hear the concern in my mother's voice, just as I did when I was my daughter's age. I remember my mother's frustrations with her daughters' seeming lack of interest in learning to cook. It is a commonly held belief in Nigeria that a woman who does not know how to cook for her husband and children has not been raised well. In other words, her lack of culinary skills reflects poorly on her mother's ability to raise a daughter. As I listen to my mother go on about why it is important for my daughter to learn how to cook for her future husband, I realize that the scene I am witnessing is probably reenacted in many other immigrant Nigerian homes. I know that I want my daughter to learn how to cook for several reasons—for basic survival and because it is cheaper and healthier than eating out. I don't expect that her culinary skills or the lack thereof should be a reflection of my measure as a mother or of hers as a well-raised woman. The reality is that she is being raised under circumstances different from mine. The cultural traditions under which I grew up may still apply to her upbringing, but with the understanding that the society in which we live demands that we confront forms of patriarchy that continue to define women by how closely they align themselves with traditional role expectations. I watch as she is caught between my mother's traditional expectations and mine, which may now be viewed by some as "Americanized" and realize that this young woman, born in Nigeria, but being raised in the United States by immigrant parents, will come to define for herself who she wants to be. Her story will be representative of the agency that second-generation immigrant children demonstrate in their ethnic identification process.

Super and Harkness (1997) have identified the family as the primary socializing influence on children. For immigrant youth, this means that they are socialized by parents who retain the language values and customs from their home country (Umana-Taylor, Bhanot, & Shin, 2006; Okpalaoka, 2009a). In spite of their efforts to transfer these customs and values to their children, immigrant parents may be up against prevailing values and customs in the United States that sometimes appear to be at odds with their own. The above story demonstrates how Nigerian immigrant families might maintain gender-specific cultural traditions as a means of protecting traditional family values.

Representative of three generations of my family living in the United States, my parents, along with my children and me, embody varying notions of what it means to be of Nigerian ascent in the United States today. While my parents have no plans to settle here permanently, my husband and I have found ourselves accepting the reality that our stay here will be longer than we initially imagined. We are raising children for whom Nigeria does not hold the same type of memories that we have. They appreciate their heritage and even celebrate its history and culture on occasion, but like many immigrants we are concerned about the retention of ethnic identity across immigrant generations (Portes & Rumbaut; cited in Dion & Dion, 2004).

The study of the complex nature of ethnic identity formation among immigrant children is not a new phenomenon (Chen, Lephuoc, Guzman, Rude, & Dodd, 2006; Alvarez, Jueng, & Liang, 2006; Vaquera & Kao, 2006; Portes & Rumbaut, 2001; Rong & Brown, 2002b; Watson, 2005; Bashi & McDaniel, 1997). What is fairly new is the interest in the ethnic identification process for recent African immigrant children, as well as children born in the United States to African immigrant parents (Okpalaoka, 2009a).

Watching my children and their peers negotiate identities as Black women in the United States raises questions as to what their experiences will be as they continue to be caught between two cultures—the culture of their parents and the culture of the receiving society in which they are being raised. These negotiations, occurring in a nation where "Blackness" continues to be defined by history (slavery) and mode and time of arrival in the United States (past or contemporary migrations) have led me to raise these questions:

1. Can my role as a bridge between three generations of African immigrants grant me the legitimacy to speak on behalf of African ascendant women from both sides of the Atlantic, and how might this inform the work that I do?
2. Even though I did not make that first transatlantic journey with my brothers and sisters, what are the possibilities of marshaling the power inherent in the fact that we are a part of each other's story despite the toll that history, distance, and experience have taken?
3. In what ways can I confront social injustices against African ascendant people in the diaspora and at the same time acknowledge that even in our shared history, our forms of struggle are not the same?

I would like to conclude with the metaphor with which I began this chapter by honoring Moraga & Anzaldúa's (1981) earlier call for women of color to bridge the differences that seek to separate us and embrace spirituality, healing, and self-recovery as necessities across our ethnicities and identities (Dillard & Okpalaoka, 2011). In so doing, I also honor my parents, who remember what once was, and my children, who are reaching for what is possible. I hope that the stories I have shared here have addressed how our lives are just one representation of the ways that African ascendant people have come to be across language, culture, and space. As we are reminded by the grandmother feminists honored here, the ways we have told our stories as African ascendants have been confining. We have to open up our understandings of the bodies we inhabited then and the ones in which we now roam the world. In the next chapter, I will take up the stories of second-generation African immigrant children like mine and the ways they engage cultural memory and the wisdom of the generations before them to maintain national voice in the diaspora.

Note

1 It was traditional practice that a child was judged to be ready for first grade (or what we called Standard One) if his or her hand could reach over the top of the head to touch the opposite ear.

Chapter 5

Cultural Memory as Endarkened Feminist Methodology

Maintaining National Voice in the African Diaspora Through (Re)membering

In the previous chapter, I narrated my family's experiences with our migrations to the United States and the ways that our stories might be representative of the various configurations of African immigrant presence in the United States. As with many immigrants, we lament what we have lost in cultural and ethnic identity in our continued sojourn here and the price we continue to pay in the tensions that persist with raising children who have to navigate what it means to be Black and of Nigerian heritage in the United States. Some of these tensions arise when our expectations of allegiance to the family ethnic identity and culture are at odds with the demands the mainstream culture makes on our children. Immigrant parents' efforts at maintaining ethnic ties to the families' national origins and their hopes that the family's culture and traditions will be passed down to future generations are not lost on their children (Okpalaoka, 2009a). The children understand what their parents' intentions are, and in choosing which aspects of the family ethnic identity and traditions to maintain, they exercise some agency in constructing their own ethnic identities (Okpalaoka, 2009a). In the past few years, we have remained hopeful. As we transition to a new phase of our lives as parents of college-age children, we have observed them actively seeking a closer identification with Africa in general and Nigeria in particular. The presence of and active participation in ethnic student organizations on campus provide an opportunity for African immigrant children who are leaving home for the first time to begin to forge their own paths in the ethnic identification process. I am reminded of Phinney's (1989) three-stage model of ethnic identity development, which is based on individual exploration of the meaning of ethnic membership and the extent to which one commits to or accepts the role that ethnic membership plays in one's life (Seaton, Scottham, & Sellers, 2006). According to Phinney (1989), the third stage of ethnic identity achievement occurs after an individual has explored what it means to be a member of an ethnic group and chooses to commit to that group. At this stage, the individual is able to assert a clear, positive sense of his or her racial or ethnic identity (Phinney, 1989). The feelings accompanying this stage are ethnic pride, belonging, and confidence. Phinney and Alipuria (1990) suggest that an achieved ethnic identity serves as a buffer against the impact of prejudice and discrimination. I observed a greater depth to my children's pride in their Nigerian roots when they became college students. Although early adolescence is when children begin to question their identity and their place in the world (Erikson, 1963; Tatum, 1997), and, as Tatum (1997) argues, "for Black youth, asking 'Who am I?' includes thinking about 'Who am I ethnically and/or racially?'" (p. 53), I found that for the Ghanaian and Nigerian girls with whom I have worked, the question of who they are ethnically and racially was further complicated by the role that their family culture and identity play in their ethnic identity formation. As it has for my daughters, college may provide the space to define who they want to be in relation to their family expectations. They can determine to what extent they want to distance themselves from or identify with their ethnic and national origins.

Well known in higher education studies for his traditional student development theories, Chickering (1969) identified seven vectors of student development, one of which is establishing identity. According to Chickering, a college student's sense of self can be measured by the extent to which the student has come to terms with who she is, where she comes from, and what she understands her life purpose to be. Later identity theorists began to examine the role that a student's race and ethnicity might play in mainstream student development theories like Chickering's. For example, McEwen, Roper, Bryant, and Langa (1990) identified factors in student development that might better suit psychosocial theories about African American college students. These include their development of ethnic and racial identity as well as cultural aesthetics, and interaction with the dominant culture. They argued that mainstream student development theories could not adequately explain the ways that ethnic minority students create a strong sense of self in college. I will argue here that cultural memory may be the missing link that could mediate the process of ethnic identity development for an ethnic minority college student.

In October 2010, I was asked by my daughter, who was president of the Association of Nigerians at a Midwestern university, to speak at the 50th-anniversary celebration of Nigeria's independence. My reflections focused on what connections to Nigeria might mean to generations of immigrant youth in the United States and in the diaspora. This talk raised a number of issues for further exploration, including: Why was the so-called "lost generation" preoccupied with celebrating the independence of a nation with which they are purported to have no close ties? Why were these young men and women commemorating a significant occasion in the nation's history, considering that they have been condemned by some to exile in the United States and viewed as least likely to return home? There are those who mourn the loss of a generation that does not appear to have enduring ties to Nigeria, but here they were, thousands of miles away from the celebrations taking place in that nation, engaged in their own process of (re)membering. What and why were these young men and women celebrating, and what role did cultural memory play in this act of (re)membering? I argue that they were reaching back to (re)member a nation to which—by familial, spiritual, and historical association—they have a connection, even if they have never set foot there. They were drawing on cultural memory to honor a nation they could lay claim to despite its remoteness.

William (2009) suggests that we not separate identity from memory, because for the African, identity does not exist outside of memory. In her book *Praisesong for the Widow,* whose central theme focuses on cultural memory and its role in our maintenance of cultural roots, Marshall (1983) captures this intertwining of identity and memory in her description of the landing of Ibo slaves in Tatem. The great aunt of the main character, Avey, draws on cultural memory to narrate the fate of Ibo slaves who were brought to the shores of Tatem. When the slaves first landed, they are said to have taken a long look around, and in their ability "to see in more ways than one" (p. 37), and being the kind of Africans who "can tell you 'bout things happened long before they was born and things to come long after they's dead" (p. 38), they walked right back into the river, choosing to rely on the memory of whence they came to escape the memory of the suffering to come. How did they know the things to come? Had they heard of the experiences of those who had made the journey before them? Whatever it was, Avey's great aunt stated that "they seen everything that was to happen 'round [there] that day" (p. 38).

In order to address the pertinent questions raised so far, it is necessary for me to look back at the role of cultural memory and (re)membering in the stories of three generations of my family represented in the United States today, and at how the link between cultural memory and identity might help explain why children who are generations removed from the history of colonial and post-colonial Nigeria thought it expedient to celebrate its 50th anniversary of independence.

First, I will define cultural memory as it is used in this chapter by borrowing from other scholarly work on the topic. Then I will situate my parents', my daughter's, and my own experiences with maintaining a connection to what Bazuin-Yoder (2011) terms our culture-of-origin, and the implications for the identity development of this immigrant generation. In doing so I hope that the reader will be able to see why and how African immigrant youth rely on cultural memory to maintain ties to their ethnic heritage in ways that are both significant and symbolic. Finally, I will forward the use of cultural memory as an endarkened feminist methodology to understand how African immigrant youth might construct varied identities in their understandings of coalition building within/across the African Diaspora, and why this should matter to those who work with them.

Defining Cultural Memory

It was in the late 1980s that Aleida and Jan Assman introduced the theory of cultural memory, distinguishing it from another memory framework, communicative memory (Erll, 2011). Although Erll (2011) argues that family memories belong mainly to the field of communicative memory, she agrees that communicative memory cannot be separated from cultural memory in the sense that both have their basis in the ways family memories, based on cultural narratives and images, shape family remembrance. Scholars of memory have been known to interchange the terms cultural, collective, and social in describing memory, but a provisional definition can be understood in cultural memory's role in "the interplay of present and past in socio-cultural contexts"

(Erll, 2008, p. 2). This definition allows us to include under this umbrella individual, group, and national acts of remembering (Erll, 2008).

Although it is an interdisciplinary subject of interest, memory is represented in the field of psychology as the ability to preserve and recall information (Halas, 2000). It has also been defined as the human capacity to remember our past by creating and recreating it (Rodriguez & Fortier, 2007). More recently, Brown (2011) defined cultural memory as "the narratives, symbols and discourses that help construct how individuals understand their place in history, as well as how past historical narratives have informed their present context" (p. 125). Brown's description of the ways that historical narratives in school texts help shape cultural memories of the past for schoolchildren can be applied to the ways that immigrant family narratives and cultural practices can help construct the cultural memories that their children hold about their ethnic and national heritage—the task that is undertaken in this chapter.

Dillard (2012) has also defined memory as "a thing, person, event that brings to mind and heart a past experience and with it, not only the ability to (re)member (to recall and think of *again*), but to also *put back together*" (p. 3; emphasis mine). When the recalled information is cultural in nature, it is referred to as cultural memory. Halas (2000) argues that memory is not exclusive to our past experiences, but is continuous in that we are making tomorrow's memories even as we recall yesterday's memories today. For Rodriguez and Fortier (2007), the purpose of cultural memory for marginalized groups is survival. Speaking of the human species, they point to the dynamism of culture as a determinant of our ability as humans to "access stored wisdom and ways of coping with diverse patterns of existence" (p. 1). I argue that for African immigrants engaged in constructing new identities in the diaspora while actively seeking to (re)member and maintain old ones, cultural memory is always in the present continuous. This means, as Dillard (2012) suggests, that memory should not be limited in its definition to just being a recalling and (re)membering of past things, but should be viewed in the context of the present continuous phrase of "putting back together." Marshall (1983) understands this very well in her description of Avey's quest "to piece together again those parts that were becoming unraveled" (Busia, 1989, p. 197). These parts, these fragments, make up "a creative and sustaining whole" (Busia, 1989, p. 197), the latter being the objective of cultural memory.

Halas (2000) supports the present nature of cultural memory in her claim that when we (re)member, we are engaging in an act that transmits reflexive knowledge about the past from the perspective of a future present. In her new book, *Learning to (Re)member the Things We've Learned to Forget*, Dillard (2012) speaks of cultural memory as the reflexive reading and (re)membering of our stories and those created by Black women in the diaspora. Using Halas's and Dillard's definitions, I suggest that cultural memory, then, is not a phenomenon that is exclusively limited to our past experiences, but is one that points toward a future present in which African ascendant people are agents in the continuous creation of new memories from old ones.

As an endarkened feminist methodology, cultural memory makes visible "the spiritual and cultural nature of (re)membering…[that helps us] appreciate the complex and contested spaces…of Black women's lives" (Dillard, 2012, p. 3). Using her memories of a marketplace experience in Ghana, when her African identity was questioned, to support the spiritual and cultural nature of remembering, Dillard (2012) describes how what might appear to be her "private and singular story" might be "representative of the collective history of African peoples," regardless of our places of settlement around the globe (p. 3). So, in order to discuss the role of cultural memory in the ways that first-, second-, and third-generation African immigrants are keeping their identification with the African continent alive, I will use a private and singular story to illustrate how my family (representative of three generations of Nigerian immigrants in the United States) have and are simultaneously (re)calling, (re)creating, and (re)living our cultural memories today, in spite of the timing of our arrival and processes of ethnic identification.

What Was Old Is New Again

I want to begin with my father's Nigeria as described by him in the stories I heard growing up. To do this, I have to go back to pre- and post-independent Nigeria, to a time when young men like my father were matriculating into and graduating out of Nigeria's premier university, the University College of London. Established in 1954, the university's tasks included grooming young men and women to take over educational and governmental positions that were gradually being vacated by the British. My father recalls an encounter at his first job after graduation with a security guard who asked him, *"You be bature?"* (this is a combination of English and Hausa that means "Are you a White man?"). The guard probably associated the college-educated men and women with the trappings of whatever he perceived the White man to be. This story reminds me of Dillard's (2006) experience in Ghana with an old woman who asked if she was a White woman. Just as this question raised issues of identity for Dillard about the "shifting ground of African identity through Ghanaian eyes" (p. 96) and marked a distinction between what the old woman saw and who Dillard was, the question my father was asked also raises issues about colonial and post-colonial identity. The guard's question simply revealed his perception that any Nigerian man or woman (of that time) who, through a university education, had acquired the accoutrements of his White educators could only naturally be White regardless of skin color. To him, White was not just a racial or biological label, but also one that was social, mental, and intellectual. I am calling up these memories from narratives I have heard from my father to help us understand the sociocultural context in which he and his peers were being educated and how this set the stage for future migrations and educational pursuits in the diaspora.

My father graduated from the university in 1963 and began work as a high school biology teacher. Upon learning that his peers were leaving the teaching field for government positions, he sought employment at the Nigerian Institute for Trypanosomiasis Research (NITR), established in 1947 as the West African Institute for Trypanosomiasis Research (WAITR) to help eradicate the tse-tse fly, which caused the sleeping sickness disease in animals and humans. In April 1964, he successfully interviewed for and began work as a junior researcher at the institute, where he soon learned of the opportunity to apply for a Rockefeller Foundation fellowship. *The Rockefeller Foundation 1964 Annual Report*, published the same year my father was awarded the fellowship, outlined the goals of the foundation, which included awareness that "newer nations and resurgent ancient states [were] painfully aware how difficult an obstacle they face[d] in the lack of people trained for the many forms of leadership and responsibility essential to national progress..." (p. 11). In their own words, "the need [was] so critical and vast that massive and coordinated effort [was] required to achieve even a moderate advance" (p. 11). These efforts led to the awarding that year of scholarship opportunities to Rockefeller Foundation fellows and scholars. My father's name is included in that report: "MICAH IKECIIUKU [sic] EZUEH B.Sc., University of Ibadan, 1963. Entomology. Appointed from West African Institute for Trypanosomiasis Research, Kaduna. Place of study: U.S.A. S-AS (Scholar-Agricultural Sciences)" (p. 165).

About 4 months later, the fellowship enabled him to pursue a graduate degree at Michigan State University, which I have discussed in more detail elsewhere in this book. African migration, at the time, was still insignificant in comparison to the increased numbers in the decades that followed; therefore, it was very important for immigrants like my father to seek out other African students. Through ethnic and social organizations, they continued to maintain ties to their home countries and to diligently uphold their national pride. These organizations were created as a means of (re)membering and maintaining a connection to their home country and building a community with those who shared similar histories and traditions. For some, these organizations were vehicles for engagement in the politics back home and contributing financially and intellectually—albeit from afar—to the national conversations.

Many African immigrants of the time returned home in anticipation of the contributions they would make to their government institutions, many of which sponsored their education abroad. However, the anticipation of taking the helm of leadership and steering the fledgling nations in new directions was fleeting. In Nigeria, the military coup of 1966 culminated in a civil war and severely interrupted the nation's social, political, and economic recovery from colonial rule. In the following decades, corrupt leadership and unstable governments stemming from the quick ascent and descent of leadership soon led to the disillusionment and corruption that still plagues many African nations today. The disillusionment with failed government coincided with the increasingly relaxed U.S. immigration policies of the 1970s, and the subsequent political and economic chaos facilitated the admission of African refugees who were fleeing civil wars and despotic regimes (Halter, 2007; Arthur, 2000).

My generation of Nigerian immigrants began arriving in the United States in the 1980s, a decade that also saw an increase in the number of legalized African immigrants, many of whom benefited from several immigration reforms. Unlike the immigrants of the 1960s and 1970s, who came to the United States primarily for education and who returned home afterward, these new immigrants came to settle and seek the American Dream. Similar to the earlier wave of African immigrants, the newcomers of the 1980s and 1990s also worked hard at maintaining a connection to their home countries through the formation of ethnic organizations and fundraising for the improvement of the communities they left behind. It was not uncommon then, as now, for these organizations to take on the task of rebuilding infrastructures such as schools, hospitals, and public libraries, and assuming social activist roles of advocating for the poor and less privileged.

When I returned to the United States in the early 1990s, I quickly connected to Nigerian social and religious communities, as did many others like me who clung to these newly formed relationships as a means of survival (Rodriguez & Fortier, 2007). These communities helped us (re)member that our cultural roots were in our home countries, and we used any opportunity we could to assemble in order to recreate customs and traditions like naming and marriage ceremonies, as well as wakes and other end-of-life events. My family quickly settled into our new lives, starting over with our careers, building new relationships, and holding on to memories of a place, culture, and time that seemed to be slipping away from us. The differences in our experiences with cultural memory have been apparent in the ways that my parents (who spend their time between Nigeria and the United States), myself (born in the United States to Nigerian immigrants, but raised primarily in Nigeria), and my children (raised their entire lives in the United States) (re)member and recreate our historical, cultural, and spiritual connections to Nigeria. My parents remember a Nigeria that is significantly different from the one in which I was raised. They can speak to the dual experience of living in the United States in two historically different times (1964–1966 and 1996–2012). Unlike me, they have both periods as a form of reference for how their lives were impacted as immigrants, how they negotiated their place and identity in their new land of sojourn, and how cultural memory served as a lighthouse, always beckoning them home.

The Nigeria in which I was raised was one that had just emerged from a civil war and quickly attained significant economic growth during the oil boom years. In 1977, the nation was so economically buoyant that it hosted the Second World Black and African Festival of Arts and Culture (FESTAC), which drew Africans from all over the continent and the diaspora. The festival attracted more than 200 leading Black scholars, whose contributions brought attention to the richness and diversity of African culture to the world (*The Black Perspective in Music*, 1977). My memories also include military coups, which seemed to come in quick succession between 1975 and 1998, even while we celebrated the nation's independence on October 1 of each year. We learned to say our pledge of allegiance to the nation at morning assembly, while we learned from old British classic authors during the day. We sang our national anthem, "Arise O compatriots, Nigeria's call obey...," while many of us exited the country in droves to seek greener pastures elsewhere. That is the Nigeria I remember when I reflect nostalgically on days gone by. Scholars who write about cultural memory are quick to caution that cultural memory is not the same as nostalgia. Nostalgia has been defined as a longing for a home that no longer exists, if it ever did (Legg, 2004), while Mazrui (2000) argues that "positive preservation of memory can become a form of nostalgia" (p. 87). Mazrui goes on to say that nostalgia is "a temporal homesickness, [an] idealizing [of] the past as our ideal home" (p. 87). The latter is not what I am doing when I remember Nigeria. Neither do I believe that the immigrant youth of whom I speak are idealizing Nigeria when they engage in cultural memory of her. One might argue that they are more likely than I to idealize a nation that may not hold the same memories for them as it does for me.

How different, then, are the experiences with cultural memory for my children and their peers? After all, they can simulate their parents' accented English in one moment and sound like their American peers in the next. They appreciate the rich texture and colors of various African fabrics, but will wear these in styles more contemporary than those of the older generation. They appreciate eating the native meals prepared in their homes, but do not necessarily want to learn how to make them. They sing and dance to a variety of contemporary African music even when they cannot identify the linguistic origin of the song. In other words, they have learned to craft an identity that is still identifiable as Nigerian or of any other African origin by retaining the core markers of the culture without losing the individuality that is a necessary part of cultural memory and maintenance.

Many of these children are aware of the economic and political challenges confronting Nigeria and other African nations. They hear about it when the adults in their lives recount their experiences during their travels home. Visiting relatives bring up-to-date accounts of the goings-on back home. With access to world news through mainstream and social media, African immigrant youth can stay current with what is happening on the continent if they so choose. They have not bought into the myth of historical Africa in which kings and queens abounded (Okpalaoka, 2009a). Instead they describe the late-night calls for financial remittance through Western Union (Okpalaoka, 2009a). Contrary to parental resignation to the fact that their children will not return to the continent to settle, some of these children speak commonly about going back to live and work on the continent (Okpalaoka, 2009a).

So, whatever efforts we see at maintaining ties to the African continent by the various African ethnic and student organizations in our communities and on our college campuses should not be attributed to idealism about the continent. The intentional efforts of African immigrant families at preserving customs, traditions, and histories of the home country and the resulting identification of their children with their families' countries of origin are commendable. It means that second- and third-generation African immigrants may feel the same connection to Africa as earlier groups of immigrants, in the ways they look back in order to look forward, by engaging their cultural memories in the production of new spaces where they can live in the fullness of what it means to be of African ascendancy (Dillard, 2012). The connection may also be evident in how they marshal new and reconstructed identities in the contexts in which they find themselves as they explore what coalitions might be built between them and those on the continent of Africa and in the diaspora. As Dillard (2012) reminds us, we (re)member in order to create the world that we want. I argue that African immigrant youth, like my daughter and her peers, in (re)membering and celebrating Nigeria's independence, are engaged in a process of creation for activism and survival as African ascendant people who are *still* committed to the well-being of their homeland.

In the next section I will continue to elaborate on the contexts in which generations of African immigrants are negotiating their identities as African ascendants in the United States and the diaspora through the (re)calling and (re)membering of African wisdom, history, and culture that cultural memory demands. I will focus on three statements that might help us understand how immigrant generational efforts at cultural preservation are passed down as cultural memory in tangible and intangible (yet authentic) ways.

Cultural Memory and (Re)created Identities

As I described earlier in this chapter, the voluntary and involuntary movement of African people all over the globe has led to the usual challenges of uprooting, settlement, and adaptation to new ways of being that rely on cultural memory to maintain ties to the homeland. Upon arrival in their new homelands, families who have migrated to improve their life and that of their children "try to adapt by seeking a balance between the need for cultural and self-continuity...and the need to adapt to the new environmental practical demands..." (Sabatier, 2008, p. 189). Speaking of African ascendants in the diaspora and their "temporary leavings," "settling ins," and "intentional movements back and forth" (p. 108) between their historical and newly gained homelands, Dillard (2012) argues that we are engaged in a continuous filling in of the blanks of our African history and memory even as we (re)produce African culture the way we (re)member it. This argument speaks to our positions of empowerment as African people to "choose particular memories and give those memories precedence in communal remembrances" (Rodriguez & Fortier, 2007, p. 12). The filling in and (re)production of African culture through remembering can be supported by the following statements.

Statement #1. African immigrant families play a significant role in their children's ethnic identity development by setting standards that are manifested through family ethnic practices. The primary motivation for maintaining sociocultural practices is to ensure cultural continuity and to ensure that their children adopt the family ethnic identity. Another way of defining the cultural continuity that these families seek can be found in the argument made by William (2009) that cultural groups invest in retaining their past to preserve their identity as well as to ensure group survival. Describing two distinct characteristics of cultural memory, Rodriguez and Fortier (2007) explain how spirituality as a form of resistance is closely connected to group survival. Therefore, we can argue that cultural memory is a spiritual act of resistance for marginalized groups that must hold on to what they can (re)member in order to survive.

Also defining the negotiation process whereby immigrant children draw from cultural resources and experiences and reconfigure these in response to time, place, and circumstance, Tsolidis (2011) emphasizes the role of the family in mediating identities between members, generations, and places. These mediated experiences may include ethnic practices associated with food and clothing, involvement in the ethnic community through membership in ethnic organizations, standards and expectations about respect for adult authority, dating, marriage, choice of peers, and, finally, academic achievement (Okpalaoka, 2009a). These are all resources that immigrant children could draw on in order to (re)member who they are, regardless of their physical distance from the continent—or to put it another way, they could use cultural resources they (re)member to construct their identities (Holland, Lachicotte, Skinner, & Cain, 1998). Referencing very early work by scholars such as Erikson (1968, 1980), Bazuin-Yoder (2011) reminds us that the experiences of our country and culture of origin affect the conscious and unconscious memories we construct and the identity stories we share.

Are parental expectations for cultural continuity tension-free? No, because African immigrant youth, like their counterparts everywhere, ask the same questions about their identity. Some feel torn between attachment to their parents' culture and peer pressure to participate in mainstream culture (Suárez-Orozco, 1999). They move across "discontinuous social spaces" as evidenced by their ability to speak one language at home, listen to African American rap with friends, and learn in mainstream English in schools (Suárez-Orozco, 1999). They are expected to retain the family language and traditional practices and at the same time assimilate into mainstream culture to the extent possible for academic and career success. This generation of African immigrants is the first to actually live in the United States at the same time as their parents. Unlike the generations before, which had grown up mostly in Nigeria and had already acquired a significant depth of knowledge of the culture and traditions before migrating as adults, this generation was mostly born in the United States or migrated at a young age. This fact is significant because it explains any tensions that might exist. In spite of the tensions, though, these children appear to be successful at negotiating ethnic and national identities that are mediated through cultural memory. Dillard (2012) cautions against marshalling "a fixed understanding of what is 'African' but instead living with/in one that is fluid, productive, and creative" (p. 111). She explains that this is the reason why African ascendant people in the diaspora can be deeply connected and influenced by the continent, even if they have never travelled to it.

Statement #2. The importance that immigrant youth place on immigrant peer relationships impacts the role of cultural memory in their joint ethnic identification process. It is apparent that forming strong relationships with peers from the same ethnic background strengthens the connection that immigrant youth feel to the African continent (Okpalaoka, 2009a). Some scholars support the link between peer friendships and adolescent identity development and the emotional and social support that accompanies such relationships (Erikson, 1968; Savin-Williams & Berndt, 1990). Peer friendships tend to arise from similarities, shared values, and aspirations (Savin-Williams & Berndt, 1990; Epstein, 1980), as supported by the findings of my study. Drawing on cultural memory, my daughter and her peers were (re)membering their shared heritage and commitment to Nigeria by celebrating through self-choreographed cultural dance, ethnic food that they collaboratively prepared, and speech and poetry that commemorated the enduring ties to their "culture-of-origin" (Bazuin-Yoder, 2011). Through cultural memory, these young men and women were borrowing from ethnic and cultural practices they had experienced and lived, and were engaged in making meaning of an African identity that is always in the process of being (re)created (Dillard, 2012). Therefore, regardless of their primary ethnic identification choices—that is, whether they identify as Nigerian, African, African-American, or American—as a cultural process they (re)member from whence they have come, helping yield insight into the place that memory holds in the (re)membering and reconfiguration of (African) identities in a transnational context (Tsolidis, 2011).

The existence of the Association of Nigerians on my daughter's campus demonstrates that Nigerian immigrant students are making conscious and strategic choices to maintain a connection to Nigeria. Although they develop friendships that cut across racial and ethnic lines, they also understand the need to stay connected to their national and historical roots through engagement with one another. They may not all have been born in Nigeria or even have visited there, but the coalition they are building with one another proves that they are becoming the voice of Nigeria in the diaspora.

In my speech to these young men and women, I encouraged them to continue to look for ways to move beyond educating the campus community about Nigeria, including adopting social justice causes in the nation. I assured them that there was much work to be done through coalition building if they assumed one voice and took up one cause at a time. I used this occasion to encourage them not to allow the strife and divisiveness that plague *our* nation today and that cripples forward movement and progress to take root in their organization. The use of the pronoun "our" was symbolic and used intentionally here to remind them that they are the future of Nigeria, regardless of where they reside in the diaspora. As I described earlier in this chapter, Nigerian immigrants born in the United States are constantly negotiating ethnic identities and loyalties between the two countries. They understand what it means to use the pronoun "our" interchangeably in reference to Nigeria and the United States in their embrace of both nations as being equally significant to their identity. That evening, I concluded my speech by asking that my audience not allow physical and temporal distance or personal politics and special interest groups to deter them from sharing a common vision for the betterment of our country.

Statement #3. The impact of personal agency on immigrant children's ethnic identification process and the extent of identification with family's country of origin cannot be overlooked. Holland and colleagues (1998) describe personal or individual agency as the power that people possess to act purposely and reflectively in situations where they or others may consider alternative courses of action. In this case, the alternative course of action for the Nigerian youth at this university might have been to let this momentous celebration in Nigerian history pass by without acknowledging or celebrating it. Another course of action might have been to separate themselves from their Nigerian identity because of some of the stereotypes that particular identity might hold. Yet they chose to align themselves with Nigeria by publicly and proudly declaring their affiliation with its history, culture, and traditions. Nigerian immigrant youth may display agency in their responses to the ways that their families and peers seek to influence their ethnic and national identities. A sense of agency is reflected in immigrant youth's conscious, deliberate decision to surrender to the fluidity of an African identity that allows each one to find her voice. To varying degrees, Nigerian immigrant youth may be similar in their picking and choosing of which aspects of their ethnic, cultural, and national identity they want to retain. This means that no two of them, even with similar backgrounds, may have the exact same notion of what a Nigerian identity means. I challenged my audience that night to (re)member that long after the night's celebration was over, each one of them would have to decide for him- or herself what being of Nigerian heritage means and the extent of their relationship with and influence in the nation that they call home.

Cultural Memory as Endarkened Feminist Methodology

The movement of African people around the world, whether through voluntary and involuntary migrations, or in response to oppression resulting from slavery and colonization, has raised questions about the identities African ascendant people adopt in their dispersion. Dillard (2012) argues that these histories have caused a fragmentation or dislocation of identities for us as a people at a level that is at once physical and spiritual. The required healing or putting back together of who we are or once were can be mediated through (re)membering. The role of cultural memory and (re)membering as endarkened responses to our experiences with geographical and historical dislocation and the fracturing of mind, spirit, and body that result from the latter is what Dillard (2012) has undertaken. She asks how (re)membering can bear witness to our individual and collective spiritual consciousness and generate new questions that can inform feminist

Cultural Memory as Endarkened Feminist Methodology 99

theory and practice. In concluding this chapter, I will suggest the following as responses to Dillard's question. These should guide the work that we do with and on behalf of African ascendant people. In order to help push the notion of (re)membering as endarkened feminist theory and practice, we need to (re)member that:

1. African ascendant people experience a collective history of movement around the globe, and even when they create home places where they have settled, they always present a spiritual connection to one another and to the continent. This connection can be attributed to the common experience of oppression, whether through slavery, colonialism, apartheid, or displacement from indigenous lands. The efforts at maintaining ties to the home country or "culture-of-origin" speak to the ways that African ascendants (re)member in order to regain/recreate identity. For endarkened feminist theory and practice, this means that we need to embrace multiple demonstrations of African identity and allow this to inform research and scholarship.

2. The connection to Africa is manifested through (re)membering that is generational in nature. This means that children of immigrants who may never have visited the home country can still feel a sense of connection that allows them to draw on cultural resources in order to (re)member. Efforts by immigrant families to inculcate ethnic, historical, and cultural allegiance to Africa in their children might appear to be futile, but through the act of (re)membering, the children create their own sense of identification that is equally legitimate. What this means for endarkened feminist theory and practice is an awareness of African immigrant youth as agents in their ethnic identification process.

3. An African identity is not static; it is fluid, contextual, and always in the process of being recreated. There is no one way of being African. Children who are raised in similar Nigerian backgrounds, for example, and who have access to similar ethnic and cultural resources from which they can draw, may adopt variants of an African identity. Rong and Brown (2002a) confirm that Black immigrants tend to move along a contin-

uum from a national origin identity to a hyphenated-American or American identity; and that although foreign-born Black youths are likely to choose a national-originated identity (e.g., Nigerian), the length of time they have spent in the United States may cause them to choose a pan-national (e.g., African) or a pan-ethnic (Black American) identity. The variation in identities is "related to different perceptions and understandings of race relations and opportunities in the United States..." (p. 259). An awareness of the fluidity of African identity allows immigrant youth to "change their mind" about who they want to be in different contexts, with the understanding that this process does not diminish their allegiance to Nigeria.

In conclusion, I have shown here that cultural memory involves agency and action, both forward-looking and future-facing notions. In describing this non-static notion of memory, William (2009) concurs that to understand memory within the construction of an African identity is to understand the relationship that exists between that which was and that which now is. Or, as best articulated by Hall, an African identity, like all identity, is continuously in the process of becoming (Hall, 1996; William, 2009). This process can only be mediated through cultural memory.

Chapter 6

"What's in a Name?"

The Names We Bear and (Im)migrant Ethnic Identity Development

In February 2013, 9-year-old Quvenzhané Wallis was nominated for an Academy Award as Best Actress for her role in the film *Beasts of the Southern Wild*. The fact that she was the youngest person ever to be nominated for a Best Actress Oscar was overshadowed by conversations surrounding the difficulty in pronouncing her name. Like many children of African ancestry who bear non-European names, Quvenzhané's experience is not unusual. Names are a significant part of our identity and impact the ways we view ourselves and the ways we are viewed by others. Our names are usually the first public identifier of who we are in our encounters with others and consequently shape others' perceptions of us (Wilson, 1998). Given to us at birth, our names carry within them the history, culture, and identity of our family heritage. The names we bear elicit stereotypical reactions in the way others treat us based on the associated expectations attached to the names (Carpusor & Loges, 2006). For recent African immigrants and African Americans in the United States and the diaspora, bearing non-European names can be a sensitive subject because of the mainly negative connotations associated with foreign-sounding names of African origin or ethnic-sounding African American names. And for their children in our schools, the regular encounters with embarrassing reactions to their names and, sometimes, outright rudeness on the part of teachers, fellow students, and total strangers, is an issue that needs to be addressed. I will draw from the existing literature as well as from my own and others' narratives to illustrate the role that African-derived names might play in the way African ascendant people feel about their ethnic identity. The results should tell us what we could learn about honoring the names we bear through an understanding of how names are inextricably tied to identity.

"Tell me your names/tell me your bashful names/and I will testify" (Lucille Clifton, 1991, p. 11)

The line above is excerpted from Lucille Clifton's poem "at the cemetery, walnut grove plantation, south carolina, 1989," in which the narrator is coaxing the slaves lying in unmarked graves to speak forth their names. The silencing that the slaves endured as a result of having their African names and identity stripped from them was a pain that they took with them to the grave. Clifton wrote this poem after she realized, on a tour of Walnut Grove, that no mention was made of the slaves who might have helped to build the plantation. Instead, she found that crosses and rocks were the only markers of the places where these men and women lay. With no names to indicate that they had ever lived and worked on the plantation, the slaves' existence had been reduced to mere sticks and stones. So, in this poem, she has chosen to "testify" on their behalf, to proclaim that they were not nameless.

Studies about naming practices allow us to examine closely social processes like identity formation and the ways our identities are linked to the names we bear (Sue & Telles, 2007). Holladay (2002) confirms that the language of names has the power to obliterate or validate our identities. For example, the act of stripping African slaves of their heritage names upon their arrival in the New World and bestowing upon them new names that they struggled to embrace was a deliberate attempt to obliterate their identities. The Trans-Atlantic Slave Trade Database lists slaves by their first names only, most of which are variations of the African names that the slaves bore at the time of their capture. The omitted surnames would have held clues to their family and ethnic heritage, but they embarked on their journey to the New World stripped of traces to ancestral roots that many would try to find in later centuries. In the same vein, the slave manifests on the National Archives website also list slaves by only one name—this time these are the first names they acquired from their owners upon arrival on U.S. shores, when they were typically given names of European origin (Dillard, 1976). Addressing slave-naming patterns in eighteenth-century Jamaica, Burnard (2001) argues against scholarship that positively depicts slave-naming patterns among slaves in the New World as being a continuation of African cultural practices. Burnard's historical account of slave naming, although focused on slave-naming practices in Jamaica, offers significant insight into what the phenomenon of slave naming might have been in the United States. His account provides us insight into the contradiction in freed slaves' rejection of slave names at the same time that they refused to reclaim African heritage names, which they considered to be inferior. Heuman (1981) also describes the phenomenon of freed slaves who, because of the shame and humiliation associated with their slave names, disposed of these as soon as possible. Yet, in a bid to be like their former owners, they refused to adopt African names and, by extension, their African heritage.

The association that Holladay (2002) makes between the names we bear and our identities is one that has been played out through centuries of involuntary and voluntary migrations to the United States. Americans have tended to view surnames as markers of ethnic origin (Waters, 1989), and the racial and social status accorded each immigrant group at various points in U.S. immigration history has determined the likelihood of members of the group retaining or changing their surnames. When they arrive in the United States, immigrants from non-English-speaking countries are confronted with the choice of holding on to their ethnic-originated names and identities or adopting new names and identities that may shield them from the disdain and contempt elicited by their ethnic heritage. Many of these immigrants have been known to shed ethnic-sounding names in favor of Anglicized names in response to the constant ridicule they experience because of their foreign names.

As recently as 2006, the Office for Civil Rights ruled that a University of Arkansas student of Nigerian origin did not have a solid case against the university, which he claimed discriminated against him on the basis of his national origin ("Student Cries Foul," 2008). The student claimed that a professor's consistent and exaggerated mispronunciation of his name elicited mockery and ridicule from his classmates, which, in turn, caused him significant humiliation. The student's complaints met some resistance from his professor and classmates, who appeared not to understand the extent of the young man's humiliation. The case was dismissed for lack of evidence.

Similarly, I have found that African immigrants with ethnic names experience varying degrees of reaction to their names (Okpalaoka, 2009a). Their foreign names are the primary indicators of their African heritage and appear to elicit some of the negative stereotypes they encounter. In some instances, bearing names that are different from commonly used names in the United States gives rise to feelings of apprehension at the prospect of being publicly addressed by name.

In this chapter I will explore how an element of shame has been historically attached to African-derived names in particular. I will demonstrate how this continues to present the bearers of such names with embarrassment when they are constantly reminded of how far removed from the commonly accepted Anglo-Saxon nomenclature their names are. First I will describe the historical experiences of immigrant groups with ethnic names and the associated reactions to those names. I hope to show how African immigrants, unlike their European counterparts, cannot evade the close scrutiny elicited by their traditional African names and their skin color, even when they adopt names of Anglo-Saxon origin.

Second, I will explicate the notion of naming in African contexts and the importance attached to the meaning behind the names that people of African ascent bear. This will serve as a background to understanding the weightiness of the naming issue for immigrants who find that names that may once have had positive connotations are now a source of shame and embarrassment.

Third, I will explore the school experiences of second-generation West African immigrant children who bear traditional African first or last names. I will explain how this might impact their school experiences and what their stories might teach us about respecting and honoring the different names that we bear. I will also include some of my own experiences as an African immigrant with first and last names that immediately separate me from the norm.

Finally, I will make recommendations from the information garnered during interviews with West African immigrant girls and from my personal experiences as to how schools might recognize the importance that all students—Black African immigrant students in particular—attach to having their names treated with respect and honored with proper pronunciation. It is hoped that educators who study issues of ethnic identity development for Black immigrant children will recognize how naming and the importance we attach to the ways our names are honored can be inextricably linked to a healthy self-identity in young children. I will propose how school officials might use the findings of this study to ensure that increasing numbers of African immigrant children and other children of color in our schools do not continue to dread roll call and the first-day-of-school practice of introducing themselves to classmates and teachers. These children should not have to Anglicize the pronunciation of their names or mumble when they are asked to speak their names. I expect that educators will understand how closely linked names and identity are and how careless reactions to African-originated names might be construed by the bearers of the names as a negation of their ethnic identity.

I will now turn to a brief background of the experiences of generations of immigrants in the United States with the ethnic names they bear in order to show how, while this phenomenon is not exclusive to African immigrants, they, unlike their European counterparts, cannot fully assimilate even when they shed nomenclatorial references to their African heritage.

History of Immigrant Experiences with Ethnic Names

Until the 1860s, almost all U.S. immigrants were from Northern and Western Europe (Stewart, 1993; Rong & Preissle, 1998; Dinnerstein & Reimers, 1999). The English—the first Europeans to establish a settlement in North America—were significant in laying the foundation for American society as we know it. The English influence on the new nation's culture was enormous—in language, institutional forms, values, and attitudes (Parrillo, 1997). Although they were a minority, the English were accorded a place of great influence in the history of the United States, and Anglo-Saxonism has remained the dominant model for newcomers to emulate (Dinnerstein & Reimers, 1999). The Anglo-Saxon influence on American society also extended to the names that later immigrants adopted. European immigrants who arrived in the 1880s understood that their predecessors had set a standard as to what was socially acceptable, including the surnames that the new immigrants were to acquire later. The newcomers' assimilation to the set Anglo-Saxon norms sometimes included taking on less ethnic-sounding surnames. Realizing that their surnames could divulge their ethnic identities and possibly impact the reception they experienced from their hosts, some immigrants adopted Anglo-Saxon variations of their surnames in order to minimize the incidence of discrimination (Waters, 1989). Describing the name-change phenomenon, Wilkerson, in *The Warmth of Other Suns: The Epic Story of America's Great Migration* (2010, p. 416 on Kindle), has this to say:

> ...with a stroke of a pen, many eastern and southern Europeans and their children could wipe away their ethnicities—and those limiting assumptions—by adopting Anglo-Saxon surnames and melting into the world of the more privileged native-born whites. In this way, generations of immigrant children could take their places without the burdens of an outsider ethnicity.... (p. 416, Loc. 8389)

Over time, descendants of European immigrants blended into mainstream White America, except in contexts where they deliberately chose to maintain a connection to their ethnic European roots. Examples of these can be found in "Little Italys" and concentrations of other ethnic groups. By the second and third generations, European immigrants were likely to have assimilated and discarded names that might reveal their ethnic heritage. The 2004 Editor's Choice Award in the Allen Ginsberg Poetry Contest was a poem written by Susan Rothbard entitled "Your Name Is Your Name." She begins the poem with the claim that the act of changing our names does not change who we are or erase our past. There will always be reminders of who we once were:

> Your name is your name, the way truth is truth.
> Even changed, it's as much a part of you as the string
> of cells that made your eyes brown and not blue.
> Years after you think you've left everything
> about your childhood behind...
> you're in a bar
> one night and find yourself face to face
> with someone from your past. And like a scar
> reopened, when she says Susan, she erases
> every word you've written. The way she says the name
> reveals what never went away: your shame. (Rothbard, 2005, p. 317)

Assimilation theorists argue that the longer immigrants live in America and intermarry with people from other cultural heritages, the more likely they are to assimilate into mainstream America, leaving their cultures and traditions behind (Gordon, 1964). Others such as Glazer and Moynihan (1970) suggest that even in the midst of assimilation, it is possible for immigrants to maintain some form of connection to their ethnic heritage. One of the ways this phenomenon is ensured is through the maintenance of ethnic names. Trueba (1999) and Trueba and Bartolome (2000) argue that immigrants manage to acquire and maintain different identities in different contexts simultaneously. They do not agree that immigrants can possibly have a simple unilinear acculturation or assimilation process from one culture to another. Rather, their resilience is the result of their ability to become an "other" and participate in different worlds. The practice of racialized renaming (Kohli & Solorzano, 2012) did not affect only African slaves and immigrants from Southern and Eastern Europe. Up until the 1920s, the indigenous people of North America had their names replaced with Anglo and Christian names (Zitkala-sa, 1921; cited in Kohli & Solorzano, 2012).

In a 2007 study, Sue and Telles examined the naming practices of Hispanic parents who gave birth to children in a Los Angeles county in 1995. They found that even though these parents gave their children English names that were translatable into Spanish, they were able to assimilate and at the same time maintain a connection to their ethnic roots. But for African American descendants of slaves and for recent African immigrants, the issue of naming was and still is a very sensitive subject, because unlike their European counterparts, they cannot blend into mainstream America even when they choose to drop their traditional African names for commonly accepted Anglo-Saxon names. Describing the experiences of Black immigrants who settled in the North during the Great Migration, Wilkerson (2010) has this to say:

> A name change would have had no effect in masking the ethnicity of black migrants.... It would have been superfluous, given that their surnames, often inherited from the masters of their forbears, were already Anglo-Saxon. They did not have the option of choosing for themselves a more favored identity. They could not assimilate whether they sought to or not. They could send their children to northern schools that were superior to anything back south, acquire a northern accent, save up for suits to replace the overalls and croker sack dresses of the field, but they would never be mistaken for an English or Welsh arriviste the way a Czech or Hungarian immigrant could if so inclined. (p. 410, Loc. 8398)

For people of African ascent, names are strongly tied to ethnic and national identity, and tensions arise when a lack of acknowledgment of personhood inherent in one's name is perceived by the bearer as an erasure of identity. This was the case in 2011 when several Baltimore lawmakers pushed to change the name of Negro

Mountain, a historical landmark, because of its reminder of a time in the nation's history when the term "Negro" was a derogatory and dehumanizing label for people of African ascent. The mountain is said to have been named in honor of a Black frontiersman who died in the French and Indian War while defending White settlers from Native Americans (Bykowicz, 2011). The fact that the mountain did not bear the hero's actual name is indicative of the erasure that has historically marked the experiences of African ascendant people. Maryland State Delegate Nathaniel Oaks argued that the failure to name the mountain after the Black frontiersman is a reminder of a time when African ascendant people were considered property and were forced to take the names of their owners (Bykowicz, 2011).

The pushback against bearing the names of former slave owners propelled the movement toward Afrocentric names as a form of resistance to European names believed to be synonymous with the former oppressors/oppressive history. This strategic move sprung out of the Civil Rights Movement of the 1960s, and for a while many African Americans adopted names that celebrated their African ancestry. Well-known examples include Malcolm Little, who later became Malcolm X, and the Black writer LeRoi Jones, who changed his name to Imamu Amiri Baraka. The Immigration Act of 1965, which opened up opportunities for Third World immigrants (Gerstle & Mollenkopf, 2001; Stewart, 1993), coincided with the Civil Rights Era and initiated noticeable African immigration to the United States. This group has largely maintained its African heritage names and has brought its naming practices to its new homeland.

Christensen (2000) cites an old Swampy Cree Indian proverb that declares, "To say a name is to begin the story" (p. 10). In the next section I will show how, in many African cultures, the story of a child's life begins with the name she is given and how this fact may explain why African immigrants tend to retain the peculiar names they bring with them to the United States, even amid the pressure to take on non-ethnic names for upward mobility.

What Is in an African Name? Pre- and Post-Immigration Experiences with Ethnic Names

Names form a significant part of our identity and may impact the stories people tell based on their perceptions of us (Wilson, 1998).

Carpusor and Loges (2006) found that "names are inherently stereotypical [and]...elicit different treatment of individuals because of the associated expectation attached to them" (p. 935). In other words, the names we bear elicit stereotypical reactions from others based on the associated expectations attached to the names (Carpusor & Loges, 2006). H. Bosmajian (1974) has compared a name to a "badge of individuality" (p. 936) and has gone as far as to claim that we have "no definition, no validity for [ourselves], without a name" (p. 936). Regardless of our cultural backgrounds, names are rarely chosen arbitrarily and may reveal everything from gender and ethnicity to religious belief and social status (Ofovwe & Awaritefe, 2009). Sue and Telles (2007) argue that the act of name selection is cultural in that names can signify the ethnic identity that parents expect for their children. These names can also have a long-term impact on the ways they influence the bearers' development of personal identities (Sue & Telles, 2007).

Among continental Africans and African immigrants in the diaspora, naming practices can be ritualistic. The intention behind name choices can be cultural and symbolic and is meant to bring a sense of purpose and meaning to the life of the bearer of the name. Because people of African heritage associate names with eventual destiny, the name a child is given at birth is meant to predict and/or determine the life outcome of that child. Even as African ascendant people move and settle around the globe, the act and art of naming remains central to their identities in their new homelands. To understand the names that African ascendant peoples bear in the diaspora and the weight behind individual decisions to embrace or discard traditional ethnic names and therefore one's ethnic heritage, it is necessary to explore how African names come to be.

Many African names position their owners in relationship to God, nature, and other people (Durand, 2001). It is not uncommon to see the recurrence of a variety of names for God in African names, and, in some instances, children are named in relationship to their living or departed relative. Traditional African names also place the owners of the names socially, geographically, and historically (Durand, 2001) and typically indicate birth order, social and historical circumstances surrounding birth, family circumstances at the time of birth, and so forth (Durand, 2001). Speaking specifically of naming practices of the Igbo people of Nigeria, Achebe (1975) claims, "if you want to know how life has treated an Igbo man, a good place to look is the names his children bear, his hopes, his fears, his joys and sorrows, his grievances against his fellows, or complaints about the way he has been used by fortune..." (p. 96).

It was colonial rule that introduced Christian and Western-derived names into the African lexicon, and even these were purposely adopted by families in hopes that the child would acquire or manifest the characteristics associated with the Biblical or historical person after whom the child was named. In many African communities today, it is not uncommon for an individual to have both traditional African and Western or Christian names.

Upon migration to Western nations such as the United States, immigrant parents may feel compelled to choose Anglo-Saxon names as the primary identifier for themselves and their offspring. This becomes especially true for the children who are born to African immigrants in the host country. African immigrants are the majority group in their countries of origin, and it is only in coming to the United States that they learn of an implicit hierarchy among minority ethnic groups that places African immigrants at the bottom of the ethnic ladder (Waters, 1994). Lieberson (2000) and Sue and Telles (2007) argue that immigrant groups who perceive themselves as the minority may be faced with two options: exchange their ethnic or native names for what they believe is an acceptable Anglo-Saxon name, or deliberately keep their native name as a form of resistance that seeks to preserve culture and tradition in their host country. Those who choose the former option do so because they believe it will make social interactions easier for their children, who will not have to experience discrimination or be taunted for having "weird" names. On the other hand, immigrants who want to preserve their history and traditions and maintain a cultural connection to their homeland tend to pick traditional names for their children. Gavigan (2010) provides other explanations for immigrant name change. She explains that immigrants may change their names in an attempt to bridge the immigrant culture with the host culture. In other instances, their new names are thrust upon them by teachers who find the immigrant children's ethnic names difficult to pronounce.

For many African immigrants, choosing Western names for their children is an attempt to limit the barriers to their children's opportunities in a society where they may already face double discrimination based on their ethnic and immigrant backgrounds. Gerhards and Hans (2009) believe that when immigrant parents give their children a name that is common in their host country, they are exhibiting a high degree of acculturation. This is arguable, especially in instances where parents understand the challenges that may arise with using native names and just want their children to fit in at school (Gavigan, 2010). Watkins and London's (1994) definition of this process as voluntary acculturation may be more accurate. On the other hand, the choice of native or traditional names for their children is indicative of ethnic maintenance on the part of immigrants (Watkins & London, 1994). So what factors compel African immigrants to react in these dually opposing ways when it comes to the names that they and their offspring adopt when they migrate to the West? The next section will address some of the consequences that people with ethnic-sounding names face when they do not conform to societal naming norms.

"I'll Just Call You by Your First Name": The Price We Pay for the Names We Bear

Most studies on names, identity, and discrimination examine the impact that names may have on the eventual social and economic status of the bearers of the names (Figlio, 2005). Some of these studies have examined the effect of ethnic-sounding names on the bearers' ability to get fair housing or a job interview (Carpusor & Loges, 2006; Bertrand & Mullainathan, 2004; Friedman & Squires, 2005). Other studies that have found a link between foreign-sounding names or non-Caucasian names and negative stereotypes include Anderson-Clark, Green, and Henley (2008), who found a relationship between ethnic names and teacher expectations for achievement. Teachers were given vignettes of fifth-grade students and instructed to judge the behavior and characteristics of the students. They found that there were significantly lower achievement scores given by raters whose descriptions used an African American–sounding name rather than a Caucasian-sounding name. Studies that have investigated how names influence attributions like intelligence, competence, ethnicity, physical attractiveness, and other positive and negative attributes include Daniel and Daniel (1998) and Hassebrauck (1988). Okpalaoka's (2009a) findings also suggest that reactions elicited by non-Caucasian names are a precursor to negative or positive stereotypes.

While most studies tend to be outcome based in their focus on how names might shape life outcomes (Edwards & Caballero, 2008), not many have addressed African immigrant children's school experiences with having foreign names and how this impacts the ways in which they self-identify ethnically, the identities that are thrust upon them by others, and how the two might shape the ways that such children navigate school cultures that remind them of their difference. Supporting the notion of difference in the school setting, Gavigan (2010) confirms that mispronunciation of a student's name by teachers and peers labels such a student as different.

According to Erikson (1963) and Tatum (1997), adolescence is the time children begin to question their identity and their place in the world. Along with trying to find their place in American society as adolescents who are Black and from African immigrant backgrounds, African immigrant children's experiences with negative reactions to their names, accented speech, and perceived inferior African heritage impact the ways they negotiate their identities in the school context. Instead of these identifiers being a source of pride to these girls, they became a source of embarrassment (Okpalaoka, 2009a). Participants in my research on ethnic identity development echoed these findings.

Madeline, who was a freshman at the time of my study, was most impacted by the reactions of her peers and teachers to her foreign last name. Although her first name is European derived, she described the taunts and discomfort that resulted from the teachers' attempts at pronouncing her last name in class. The fact that Madeline was an adolescent girl at the time of this study is significant because, at this stage of development, adolescents tend to be self-conscious and aware of the ways in which they are different from their peers. Madeline's predicament is not uncommon, even among adult immigrants like me, as illustrated in the short narrative below.

I went to the bakery on my daughter's fifth birthday to pick up a cake I had ordered. And like I have done on innumerable occasions, I spelled out my last name as soon as the bakery attendant asked for it to help her retrieve the right cake. In response she said, "I remember that weird name." I thought of a very quick and appropriate response, but I bit my tongue, picked up my cake, and left the store. As I walked away, I reflected on the awkwardness that always accompanies the announcement of my name. Chinwe—C-h-i-n-w-e. Okpalaoka—O-k-p-a-l-a-o-k-a. It is almost automatic the way I begin to spell each time I am asked for my name. I don't only say it, but I begin to spell it. It is as if I am trying to quickly minimize the awkwardness of having such an unusual name, and I think, "Maybe if I spell it very quickly, both of us will be spared the discomfort of the moment." I also remember my apprehension during a roll call in the summer of 1991 as I sat in training for a new job, because I knew that the young manager would stumble when he came to my name. I had only been in the United States for a few months and already knew that a name I had taken for granted until now would henceforth carry within it many meanings and perceptions that the hearer of the name would chose to ascribe to it. I know what it is for people to say "I am not even going to try to say your name" or "I'll just call you by your first name." I understand the struggle that my own children experience in school with having foreign last names. At my 8-year-old daughter's school, the principal makes daily birthday announcements over the PA system by calling out the names of students whose birthdays fall on that day. Recently, my daughter shared how, on her birthday, she "went" to the bathroom at the time she knew the names were about to be announced because she did not want to watch her classmates' reactions to the principal's clumsy pronunciation of her first and last names. She was sharing this experience many months after it had taken place, and I wondered how many other times she had reacted with embarrassment at the pronunciation of her name and kept the experience to herself. I naturally turned this into a lesson on how special her name was and how difficult it was for non-speakers of Igbo, the linguistic origin of her name, to capture the exact pronunciation of her name. I tried to help her understand that this is a predicament that she will continue to face in school and life.

Madeline's story, in the next section, describes her experiences as a high school student and highlights how the feelings that accompany the dishonoring of our names can extend beyond the early years of schooling and, in my case, into adulthood.

"What Happened to Your Last Name?"
A Tale of Naming, Shaming, and Identity

"Your last name is weird. Where are you from?" (Madeline, personal interview, February 11, 2008)

At the time I met Madeline, she was a 16-year-old high school sophomore who was born on the East Coast to Ghanaian immigrants but was now living and attending school in the Midwest. Her family migrated to the United States in 1989 and lived on the East Coast for about 9 years before moving to the Midwest. Madeline's father was the first in the family to migrate, and her mother joined him after he filed for and obtained immigration papers for her. Hondagneu-Sotelo (1992) has referred to this process in immigration as "family stage migration," an immigration pattern that occurs when a spouse migrates to seek work without the other spouse and children, who join him or her later.

Madeline revealed a remarkable ability to wield contextual identities, switching from a Ghanaian identity to an African American one after identifying as Ghanaian caused her to be embarrassed by her ethnic background. I concluded that her reaction was attributable to her peers' response to her heritage. She described encounters with her classmates whose knowledge of Africans was that of poverty and hunger. She understood that her peers initially perceived her to be African American and that it was her surname that gave away her ethnic background. Although some scholars argue that physical features and skin color can give away the identity of African immigrants (Bashi & McDaniel, 1997), this is not always so, as we see in Madeline's case. When her schoolmates find out about her African background, they usually respond negatively by asking her "weird" questions like: "Whoa! I thought you [were] African American. What happened to your last name?" Madeline confided that, at those times, she has wished that she was from a background other than Ghanaian. Sometimes she has pleaded with her parents, "Can we please change our last name?"

As I have described above, the foreign last name was one of the factors that attracted attention to Madeline's African heritage and consequently elicited stereotypical comments from her peers. Although Madeline was a high school sophomore at the time of this study, she still recalled an experience that took place in fifth grade. On hearing the teacher mispronounce her last name, a classmate remarked, "Eww, she's from Africa. She needs to go back where she came from." Saddened by this experience, Madeline reported the incident to her parents, who came to school to meet with the student.

Although Madeline reported that the incidents involving the mispronunciation of her last name lessened as she entered high school, the memories of her fifth-grade experience have remained with her. Remembering how difficult that time was for her, Madeline recounted:

> I would cry and go home and I'll be like, "Why are we Africans for?" and "All this stuff is not fair..." It was really difficult for me during that time, because people didn't understand that—because all they think about is like, "Africa is poor so [I am] probably from a poor country." (personal interview, February 11, 2008)

To emphasize how important it was for her that her last name be pronounced correctly, Madeline shared her fears about graduation, which was 2 years away from the time of the study. Speaking of her fear of having her last name mispronounced at graduation and the attention it would attract, Madeline said:

> Because [my last name] is so long and I don't want to struggle and when I get my diploma, they'll be like, "Madeline... [long pause]." Yeah, I don't wanna walk across the stage and everybody's laughing at me and they mess up my pronunciation. That's the biggest fear I have right now is pronouncing my last name. (personal interview, February 11, 2008)

Madeline's statements may appear to some to be a minor issue, but for a girl who was at an impressionable stage of adolescent development, it mattered enough to cause her to want a different name and identity. Like my elementary-age daughter, who knew that excusing herself to go to the bathroom in second grade would spare her the embarrassment of hearing her name mispronounced over the PA system, Madeline was aware of what the snickering of her classmates meant to her self-esteem. Children with uncommon names are subjected to ridicule by their peers (Kohli & Solorzano, 2012), and when we do not take the time to learn the correct pronunciation of children's names, we are contributing to the problem. What role could the school play in the experiences of

Madeline and children like her, for whom ethnic names are a source of unwanted attention?

First of all, since getting to know the names of the students in her class is a common first-day-of-school occurrence for teachers, it is important that the teacher ask to be taught the proper pronunciation of a student's name without drawing attention to the student. Even when students' names have a more commonly used pronunciation, the teacher should be attentive to the way each child wants to be addressed. In her article "The First Day of Class: How It Matters," Shadiow (2009) describes a first-day-of-school experience as a novice teacher that shaped subsequent first-day-of-school interactions with her class. At age 22, she had arrived at her first classroom with a teacher-centered narrative of the way things would play out in her classroom. She describes how a young male student's introduction of himself to her shifted her focus from herself to that of being learner centered. Drawing from Noddings's ethic of care (1999, 2002), Shadiow learned the importance of educators asking if an act has helped or hindered an interaction with a student. Teachers who understand the vulnerability that children bring with them to the school context and their innate need for peer acceptance can help alleviate the anxiety associated with having names that are different.

The prejudices and stereotypes that immigrants and native-born students of color experience have been shown to affect their self-esteem, mental health, and academic achievement (Gay, 2000; Kohli & Solorzano, 2012). I argue that such prejudices and stereotypes include people's reactions to the names that we bear. For Black African immigrant children who have to contend with negative stereotypes about Africa, having a non-Europeanized name only adds to the existing narrative of Africans as backward, primitive, and uncivilized. Kohli and Solorzano (2012) have described the cultural disrespect that students of color face with regard to their names as racial microaggression. Because these "subtle daily insults...support a racial and cultural hierarchy of minority inferiority," they might go unnoticed by others (p. 441). They go on to say that the mispronunciation of names for these students is perceived by them as a devaluation of their cultural heritage.

Second, based on their qualitative study of 41 participants of ethnically diverse backgrounds, Kohli and Solorzano (2012) found that teachers and other students were consciously or unconsciously complicit in a cultural "othering" of students with foreign and ethnic names. They concluded that this negated the goals of maintaining a multicultural school environment. How can the issue of names be taken up as part of a multicultural dialogue? After the Immigration Reform Act of 1965, the surge in immigration raised the question of the best ways to school immigrant children. Banks and Banks (2005) describe multicultural education as education that "incorporates the idea that all students—regardless of their gender and social class and their ethnic, racial, or cultural characteristics—should have an equal opportunity to learn in school" (p. 3). They add: "some students, because of these characteristics, have a better chance to learn in schools as they are currently structured than do students who belong to other groups or who have different cultural characteristics" (p. 3). Banks and Banks (2005) argue that a school curriculum that focuses on the experiences of mainstream Americans and ignores the experiences, cultures, and histories of other ethnic, racial, cultural, language, and religious groups has negative effects on both majority and minority students. Immigrant children are at a disadvantage when they arrive in U.S. schools because they are different. The differences can be physical, cultural, religious, or linguistic—or, as in the case of this chapter, nomenclatural. Native-born students and teachers are uncomfortable with unfamiliar languages, names, foods, dress, customs, and smells. Schools already address some of these issues by celebrating different ethnicities through international fairs and celebrations and talks by guest speakers who are members of the immigrant community. Perhaps celebrating the diversity of names and maintaining a proactive rather than a reactive stance in addressing the rich history and culture of the school population in general and the names we bear in particular is a step in the right direction. Ladson-Billings (2001) concludes that culturally competent teachers not only understand the role of culture in education; they also ignore existing cultural distortions and stereotypes by learning about their students' cultural backgrounds. In so doing, the classroom context is moved from being a place of "othering" to a place of empowerment of learning as teacher and students become co-learners in a complex but rewarding environment that spans racial, ethnic, cultural, historical, and national boundaries.

I will end by noting that as Black children navigate the various stages of identity development (Cross, 1995; Phinney, 1989; Helms, 1990), it is possible for them to achieve positive ethnic identities to the extent that the embarrassment they experience with having ethnic names disappears and is replaced by mere irritation. Whether it is during (1) the internalization stage (Cross, 1995), when a new, more balanced, and authentic racial identity that is salient to Blackness is formed and integrated into the individual's life; (2) Helms's (1990) internalization-integrative awareness stage, when the individual values his own culture and others' and seeks to understand and take action on behalf of both; or (3) Phinney's ethnic identity achievement stage (Phinney, 1989), when the individual is able to assert a clear, positive sense of his or her ethnic identity accompanied by ethnic pride, belonging, and confidence, it is important to consider that there is no single model or response to the issues raised in this chapter about naming. Therefore, teachers should take racial and ethnic identity development stages into consideration as they respond to students' needs for recognition and validation. There is no limit to the age at which we want our ethnic names and cultural backgrounds to be valued and honored, just as there is no monolithic response to the issue of ethnic names. All people want to know is that they are seen and heard. So when a student says, "That is not how to say my name," the response "Whatever!" or the act of continually mispronouncing the student's name dismisses not only the student's concerns, but can be said to be dismissive of the student herself.

Epilogue

"What Nation You Is?"

Negotiating Diaspora and African Identities—Which Way Forward?

Following the previous chapter on the significance of naming to the identities we carry as African ascendant people in the diaspora, I would like to revisit the term African "ascendant" as made popular by Dillard (2006, 2012) and used to capture the movements of African people in the world. The play on the word "ascend" connotes an upward, progressive movement: always in motion, always fluid, and always becoming. As far back as has been documented by historians, African people have been on the move, sometimes of their own volition but historically as a result of forced removal from the place they call or once called home. As we have settled around the world, successive generations of Africans have assumed hybrid identities made possible through assimilation, marriage, citizenship, or birth. So whether the place of settlement is in the Caribbean, the U.K., Canada, or the United States, many can trace their ancestry to Africa in ways that allow each of us to define the extent of our connection to the continent. Whereas some African ascendant people can make immediate connections to specific regions or people groups, others have no traceable connection to their African roots.

I began this book with the question "Who is an African?" This is the quintessential question in the sometimes-complicated inter- and intra-group relationships in which African peoples find themselves. This question is taken up in the various social, national, political, and educational contexts. It is asked in our schools in interactions between African immigrant children and their African American peers. It is a question that continental Africans ask of contemporary African immigrants in the diaspora. Even when it is asked differently, the intent of the question seems to be the same—to include or exclude and to ascertain who can rightfully claim that identity, considering the many different and yet legitimate ways that African identity is being marshaled in the world.

"What's your nation? Which nation you is?" asks Lebert Joseph in Paule Marshall's *Praisesong for the Widow* (1983). Every year, during the Beg Pardon dance, Joseph returns to Carriacou to celebrate the memory of the "Old Parents," the ancestors who are believed to still have the power either to bless or withhold blessings from those they have left behind. During the nation dances, ascendants of each nation dance in celebration of their ancestral nation of origin. Names like Temne, Banda, Cromanti, and Congo are announced so that those who remember can get up and dance to the ancestors, pleading for their intervention in the lives of their living ascendants. As Avey watched,

> It was the essence of something rather than the thing itself she was witnessing.... All that was left were the few names of what they called nations which they could no longer even pronounce properly, the fragments of a dozen or so songs, the shadowy forms of long-ago dances and rum kegs for drums. (Marshall, 1983, p. 240)

For those who did not know their nation or who could not trace their national lineage, Lebert Joseph said:

> when you see me down on my knees at the Big Drum singing the Beg Pardon, I don' be singing just for me one. Oh no! Is for *tout moun'*.... I has all like you in mind. 'Cause you all so that don' know your nation can't take part when the Beg Pardon or the nation dances is going on.... The Old Parents would be vex. (p. 175)

Knowing one's nation of origin regardless of time and mode of arrival in the United States or anywhere else and its impact on identity has been taken up throughout this book. I do not claim to have captured the stories of every African ascendant person in the diaspora. I have relied on mine and my family's stories, the stories of Ghanaian and Nigerian girls with whom I have worked, and a review of what is currently available in the literature. Whether in the questions raised about President Barack Obama's "Blackness" or those raised in my study about what an African looks and sounds like, it is time that we pay attention to an issue that is here to stay: The ways we teach Black children and do research with and on their behalf may no longer work. We have to reconsider our teaching and research methodologies by discarding monolithic perceptions of all Black people or all African immigrants. We do this by taking into account how slavery, colonialism, and other forms of oppression have muddied not only the literal waters of Africa, but also our predisposition to put people into neat little identity boxes. In so doing, teachers, educators, and scholars alike can say, like Lebert Joseph, *I don' be singing just for me one. Oh no! Is for tout moun'.... I has all like you in mind.*

References

Achebe, C. (1960). *No longer at ease*. London: Heinemann.

———. (1966). *A man of the people*. New York: Anchor Books.

———. (1969). *Arrow of God*. New York: Anchor Books.

———. (1975). *Morning yet on creation day*. London: Heinemann.

———. (1992). Interview. In A.K. Appiah (Ed.), *In my father's house: Africa in the philosophy of culture*. New York: Oxford University Press.

———. (2000). *Things fall apart*. London: Heinemann. (Original work published 1958).

———. (2013). *There was a country: A personal history of Africa*. New York: Penguin.

Adeyanju, C.T., & Oriola, T.B. (2011). Colonialism and contemporary African migration: A phenomenological approach. *Journal of Black Studies, 42*(6), 943–967.

Adibe, J. (Ed.). (2009). *Who is an African? Identity, citizenship and the making of the African nation*. London: Adonis and Abbey.

Aidoo, A. (1998). The African woman today. In. O. Nnaemeka (Ed.), *Sisterhood: Feminisms and power—From Africa to the Diaspora*. Trenton, NJ: Africa World Press.

Alexander, M.J. (2005). *Pedagogies of crossing: Meditations on feminism, sexual politics, memory, and the sacred*. Durham, NC: Duke University Press.

Alvarez, S., Friedman, E.J., Beckman, E., Blackwell, M., Chinchilla, N.S., Lebon, N., et al. (2002). Encountering Latin American and Caribbean feminisms. *Signs: Journal of Women in Culture & Society, 28*(2), 537–579.

Alvarez, A., Jueng, L., & Liang, C. (2006, July). Asian-Americans and racism: When bad things happen to "model minorities." *Cultural Diversity and Ethnic Minority Psychology, 12*(3), 477–492.

Amole, B. (1992). The boys quarters: An enduring legacy in Nigeria. In A. Arisitidis, C. Karaletsou, & K. Tsoukala (Eds.), *Socio-environmental metamorphoses*. Proceedings of the 12th International Conference of the IAPS, Chalkidikik, Greece, July 11–14, 1992.

Anderson-Clark, T.N., Green, R.J., & Henley, T.B. (2008). The relationship between first names and teacher expectations for achievement motivation. *Journal of Language & Social Psychology, 27*(1), 94–99.

Anzaldúa, G. (1987). *Borderlands/La frontera: The new mestiza*. San Francisco, CA: Spinsters/Aunt Lute.

Anzaldúa, G., & Keating, A. (2002). *This bridge we call home: Radical visions for transformation*. New York: Routledge.

Appiah, K.A. (1992). *In my father's house: Africa in the philosophy of culture.* New York: Oxford University Press.

———. (2006). *Cosmopolitanism: Ethics in a world of strangers.* New York: W.W. Norton.

Armah, A.K. (1968). *The beautyful ones are not yet born.* Boston, MA: Houghton Mifflin.

———. (1969). *Fragments.* London: Heinemann.

———. (1973). *Two thousand seasons.* London: Heinemann.

Arthur, J. (2000). *Invisible sojourners: African immigrant diaspora in the United States.* Westport, CT: Praeger.

Azuah, U. (2005). *Sky high flames.* Frederick, MD: PublishAmerica.

Babou, C.A. (2008). Migration and cultural change: Money, "caste," gender, and social status among Senegalese female hair braiders in the United States. *Africa Today,* 55(2), 3–22.

Banks, J.A. (1993). Multicultural education for young children: Racial and ethnic attitudes and their modification. In B. Spodek (Ed.), *Handbook of research on the education of young children* (pp. 236–250). New York: Macmillan.

———. (Ed.). (1996). *Multicultural education, transformative knowledge and action.* New York: Teachers College Press.

———. (Ed.). (1997). *Educating citizens in a multicultural society.* New York: Teachers College Press.

Banks, J.A. & Banks, C. (2005). *Multicultural education: Issues and perspectives* (5th ed.). Hoboken, NJ: John Wiley & Sons.

Bashi, V., & McDaniel, A. (1997). A theory of immigration and racial stratification. *Journal of Black Studies,* 27(5), 668–682.

Bazuin-Yoder, A. (2011). Positive and negative childhood and adolescent identity memories stemming from one's country and culture-of-origin: A comparative narrative analysis. *Child Youth Care Forum, 40,* 77–92.

Bell-Scott, P. (1994). *Life notes: Personal writings by contemporary Black women.* New York: W.W. Norton & Company.

Bennett, L. (1984). *Before the Mayflower: A history of Black America.* New York: Penguin.

Berlin, I. (2003). *Generations of captivity: A history of African-American slaves.* Cambridge: Belknap Press of Harvard University Press.

Bertrand, M., & Mullainathan, S. (2004). Are Emily and Greg more employable than Lakisha and Jamal? A field experiment on labor market discrimination. *American Economic Review, 94,* 991–1013.

The Black Perspective in Music. (1977). 5(1), 104–117.

Bosmajian, H. (1974). *The language of oppression*. Washington, DC: Public Affairs.

Brown, E.R. (2005). Decentering dominant discourses in education: The emancipatory possibilities of our work. In F. Bodone (Ed.), *What difference does research make and for whom?* New York: Peter Lang.

Brown, K. (2011). Race, racial cultural memory and multicultural curriculum in an Obama "post-racial" U.S. *Race, Gender & Class, 18*(3/4), 123–134.

Burnard, T. (2001). Slave naming patterns: Onomastics and the taxonomy of race in eighteenth century Jamaica. *Journal of Interdisciplinary History, 31*(3), 325–346.

Busia, A.P.A. (1989). What is your nation? Reconnecting Africa and her Diaspora through Paule Marshall's *Praisesong for the widow*. In C.A. Wall (Ed.), *Changing our own words: Essays on criticism, theory, and writing by Black women* (pp. 196–211). New Brunswick, NJ: Rutgers University Press.

Bykowicz, J. (2011, February 20). Controversy over "Negro mountain" reveals urban-rural divide. *The Baltimore Sun*. Retrieved from http://articles.baltimoresun.com

Caldarella, P., Adams, M., Valentine, S., & Young, K.R. (2009). Evaluation of a mentoring program for elementary school students at risk for emotional and behavioral disorders. *New Horizons in Education, 57*(1), 1–16.

Cameron, J. (1999). *The right to write*. NY: Tarcher/Putnam.

Carpusor, A.G., & Loges, W. (2006). Rental discrimination and ethnicity in names. *Journal of Applied Social Psychology, 36*(4), 934–952.

Cayleff, S., Herron, M., Cormier, C., Wheeler, S., Chavez-Arteaga, A., Spain, J., & Dominguez, C. (2011). Oral history and "Girl's voices": The Young Women's Studies Club as a site of empowerment. *Journal of International Women's Studies, 12*(4), 22–44.

Césaire, A. (1955). Between colonizer and colonized. In C. Lemert (Ed.), *Social theory: The multicultural and classic readings* (2nd ed.). Boulder, CO: Westview Press.

Chen, G., Lephuoc, P., Guzman, M., Rude, S., & Dodd, B. (2006). Exploring Asian-American racial identity. *Cultural Diversity and Ethnic Minority Psychology*, 12(3), 461–476.

Chickering, A. (1969). *Education and identity*. San Francisco, CA: Jossey-Bass.

Christensen, D. (2000). *Ahtahkakoop: The epic account of a Plains Cree head chief, his people, and their struggle for survival, 1816–1896*. Shell Lake, Saskatchewan: Ahtahkakoop Publishing.

Chuku, G. (2005). *Igbo women and economic transformation in southeastern Nigeria, 1900–1960*. New York: Routledge.

Clifton, L. (1991). at the cemetery, walnut grove plantation, south carolina, 1989. In *Quilting: Poems, 1987–1990*. Brockport, NY: BOA Editions.

Collins, P.H. (1990). *Black feminist thought: Knowledge, consciousness, and the politics of empowerment*. New York: Routledge.

———. (2000). *Black feminist thought: Knowledge, consciousness, and the politics of empowerment* (2nd ed.). New York: Routledge.

———. (2003). Toward an Afrocentric feminist epistemology. In Y.S. Lincoln & N.K. Denzin (Eds.), *Turning points in qualitative research: Tying knots in a handkerchief*. Walnut Creek, CA: AltaMira Press.

Contreras, A. (2002). The impact of immigration policy on education reform: Implications for the new millennium. *Education and Urban Society, 34*(2), 134–155.

Crichlow, W., Goodwin, S., Shakes, G., & Swartz, E. (1990). Multicultural ways of knowing: Implications for practice. *Journal of Education, 172*(2), 101–117.

Cross, W. (1995). The psychology of Nigrescence: Revising the Cross model. In J. Ponterotto, J. Casas, L. Suzuki, & C. Alexander (Eds.), *Handbook of multicultural counseling* (pp. 93–122). Thousand Oaks, CA: Sage.

Cummings, C. (2003). Tracing the trade routes of the slaves. *The Western Scholar*, pp. 1–5.

Daniel, E., & Daniel, L. (1998). Preschool children's selection of race-related personal names. *Journal of Black Studies,* 28, 471–491.

Danticat, E. (1996). *Krik? Krak!* New York: Vintage Books.

Das, A.K. & Kemp, S.F. (1997). Between two worlds: counseling South Asian Americans. *Journal of Multicultural Counseling and Development,* 25, 23–33.

Dasgupta, S.D. (1998). Gender roles and cultural continuity in the Asian Indian immigrant community in the United States. *Sex Roles,* 38, 953–973.

Dillard, C.B. (2000). The substance of things hoped for, the evidence of things not seen: Examining an endarkened feminist epistemology in educational research and leadership. *International Journal of Qualitative Studies in Education, 13,* 661–681.

———. (2006). *On spiritual strivings: Transforming an African American woman's academic life*. Albany: State University of New York Press.

———. (2012). *Learning to (re)member the things we've learned to forget: Endarkened feminisms, spirituality, and the sacred nature of research and teaching*. New York: Peter Lang.

Dillard, C.B., & Okpalaoka, C.L. (2011). The sacred and spiritual nature of transnational Black feminist praxis in qualitative research. In N.K. Denzin & Y.S. Lincoln (Eds.), *The Sage handbook of qualitative research* (4th ed.). Los Angeles, CA: Sage.

Dillard, C.B., Abdur-Rashid, D., & Tyson, C.A. (2000). My soul is a witness: Affirming pedagogies of the spirit. *International Journal of Qualitative Studies in Education, 13*, 447–462.

Dillard, J.L. (1976). *Black names.* The Hague: Mouton.

Dion, K.K., & Dion, K.L. (1996). Cultural perspectives on romantic love. *Personal Relationships, 3*, 5–17.

———. (2004). Gender, immigrant generation and ethnocultural identity. *Sex Roles, 50*(5/6), 347–355.

Dinnerstein, L., & Reimers, D. (1999). *Ethnic Americans: A history of immigration* (4th ed.) New York: Columbia University Press.

Dixon, M. (2005). Hair braiding: Working the boundaries of methodology in globalisation research [online]. *Qualitative Research Journal, 5*(1), 80–89.

Djamba, Y. (1999). African immigrants to the United States: A socio-demographic profile in comparison to native Blacks. *Journal of Asian and African Studies, 34*(2), 210–215.

Durand, G. (2001). The survival of names of African origin in Martinique after emancipation. *Dialectical Anthropology, 26*, 193–233.

Edmonston, B., & Passel, J.S. (1992). *Immigration and immigrant generations in population projections.* Washington, DC: Urban Institute.

Edwards, R., & Caballero, C. (2008). What's in a name? An exploration of the significance of personal naming of 'mixed' children for parents from different racial, ethnic and faith backgrounds. *The Sociological Review*, 56(1), 39–60.

Ellis, C., & Bochner, A. (2003). Autoethnography, personal narrative, reflexivity: Researcher as subject. In N. Denzin & Y. Lincoln (Eds.), *Collecting and interpreting qualitative materials.* Thousand Oaks, CA: Sage.

Ellis, C., & Ginsburg, R. (Eds.). (2010). *Cabin, quarter, plantation: Architecture and landscapes of North American slavery.* New Haven, CT: Yale University Press.

Eluwa, G.I.C., Ukagwu, M.O., Nwachukwu, J.U.N., & Nwaubani, A.C.N. (1988). *A history of Nigeria.* Onitsha: Africana-FEP Publishers.

Epstein, S. (1980). The self-concept: A review and the proposal of an integrated theory of personality. In E. Staub (Ed.), *Personality: Basic issues and current research* (pp. 82–132). Englewood Cliffs, NJ: Prentice-Hall.

Erikson, E.H. (1963). *Childhood and society.* New York: Norton. (Original work published 1950).

———. (1968). *Identity, youth and crisis.* New York: Norton.

———. (1980). *Identity and the life cycle.* New York: W.W. Norton & Co.

Erll, A. (2008). Cultural memory studies: An introduction. In A. Erll & A. Nunning (Eds.), *Cultural memory studies: An interdisciplinary handbook* (pp. 1–19). Berlin and New York: de Gruyter.

———. (2011). Locating family in cultural memory studies. *Journal of Comparative Family Studies, 42*(3), 303–318.

Fanon, F. (1967). The fact of Blackness. *Black skin, White masks.* New York: Grove Press.

Fernandes, L. (2003). *Transforming feminist practice: Non-violence, social justice and the possibilities of a spiritualized feminism.* San Francisco: Aunt Lute Books.

Figlio, D.N. (2005). *Names, expectations and the Black-White test score gap.* NBER Working Paper No.W11195. Cambridge, MA: National Bureau of Economic Research.

Fischler, L., & Zachary, L. (2009). Shifting gears: The mentee in the driver's seat. *Adult Learning, 20*(1/2), 5–9.

Foner, N. (1987). The Jamaicans: Race and ethnicity among migrants in New York City. In N. Foner (Ed.), *New immigrants in New York* (pp. 131–158). New York: Columbia University Press.

Fontana, A., & Frey, J. (2003). The interview: From structured questions to negotiated text. In N.K. Denzin & Y.S. Lincoln (Eds.), *Collecting and interpreting qualitative materials* (pp. 61–106). Thousand Oaks, CA: Sage.

Fordham, S. (1996). *Blacked out: Dilemmas of race, identity and success at Capital High.* Chicago: University of Chicago Press.

Fordham, S., & Ogbu, J. (1986). Black students' school success: Coping with the burden of "acting white." *Urban Review, 18,* 176–206.

Freire, P. (1970). *Pedagogy of the oppressed.* New York: Herder and Herder.

———. (1992). *Pedagogy of hope.* New York: Continuum.

———. (2000). *Pedagogy of the oppressed.* New York: Continuum.

Friedman, S., & Squires, G.D. (2005). Cybersegregation: *Is Neil Kelly a more desirable tenant than Tyrone Jackson or Jorge Rodriguez? A research proposal.* Conference Papers, American Sociological Association, 2005 Annual Meeting, Philadelphia, 1–9.

Fuligni, A., Witkow, M., & Garcia, C. (2005). Ethnic identity and the academic adjustment of adolescents from Mexican, Chinese, and European backgrounds. *Developmental Psychology, 41*(5), 799–811.

Gavigan, K. (2010). *What's in a name? Honoring students' cultural identities.* Library Media Connection, 29(3), 26–27.

Gay, G. (2000). *Culturally responsive teaching: Theory, research & practice.* New York: Teachers College Press.

Gerhards, J., & Hans, S. (2009). From Hasan to Herbert: Name-giving patterns of immigrant parents between acculturation and ethnic maintenance. *American Journal of Sociology, 114*(4), 1102–1128.

Gerstle,, G., & Mollenkopf, J. (2001) (Eds.). The political incorporation of immigrants, then and now. In *E Pluribus Unum?: contemporary and historical perspectives on immigrant political incorporation*. NY: Russell Sage Foundation.

Gibau, G. (2005). Contested identities: Narratives of race and ethnicity in the Cape Verdean diaspora. *Identities: Global Studies in Culture and Power, 12*, 405–438.

Gilroy, P. (1993). *The Black Atlantic: Modernity and double-consciousness*. New York and London: Verso.

Glazer, N., & Moynihan, D.P. (1970). *Beyond the melting pot: The Negroes, Puerto Ricans, Jews, Italians, and Irish of New York City*. (2nd ed.). Massachusetts: The MIT Press.

Gordon, M. (1964). *Assimilation in American life*. NY: Oxford University Press.

Gordon, A. (1998). The new diaspora: African immigration to the United States. *Journal of Third World Studies, 15*(1), 79–103.

Grant, C.M., & Simmons, J.C. (2008). Narratives on experiences of African-American women in the academy: Conceptualizing effective mentoring relationships of doctoral student and faculty. *International Journal of Qualitative Studies in Education, 21*(5), 501–517.

Guion, L.A., Diehl, D.C., & McDonald, D. (2002). *Triangulation: Establishing the validity of qualitative studies*. University of Florida IFAS Extension. Retrieved from https://edis.ifas.ufl.edu/pdffiles/FY/FY39400.pdf

Halas, E. (2000). Time and memory: A cultural perspective. *TRAMES: A Journal of the Humanities and Social Sciences, 14*(4), 307–322.

Hall, S. (1996). Who needs identity? In S. Hall & P. Du Gay (Eds.), *Questions of cultural identity* (pp. 1–17). London: Sage.

Halter, M. (2007). Africa: West. In M. Waters & R. Ueda (Eds.), *The new Americans: A guide to immigration since 1965*. Cambridge, MA: Harvard University Press.

Hassebrauck, M. (1988). Beauty is more than "name" deep: The effect of women's first names on ratings of physical attractiveness and personality attributes. *Journal of Applied Social Psychology, 19*, 721–726.

Helms, J. (1990). *Black and White racial identity: Theory, research, and practice*. New York: Greenwood Press.

———. (1995). An update of Helms's white and people of color racial identity models. In J. Ponterotto, J. Casas, L. Suzuki, & C. Alexander (Eds.), *Handbook of multicultural counseling* (pp. 181–198). Thousand Oaks, CA: Sage.

Henderson, T.L., Hunter, A.G., & Hildreth, G.J. (2010). Outsiders within the academy: Strategies for resistance and mentoring African American women. *Michigan Family Review, 14*(1), 28–41.

Hesse-Biber, S.N. (2006). The practice of feminist in-depth interviewing. In S. N. Hesse-Biber & P.L. Leavy (Eds.), *Feminist research in practice: A primer.* Thousand Oaks, CA: Sage Publications.

Heuman, G.J. (1981). *Between Black and White: Race, politics, and the free coloreds in Jamaica, 1792–1865.* Westport, CT: Greenwood Press.

Holladay, H. (2002). Black names in white space: Lucille Clifton's South. *Southern Literary Journal, 34*(2), 120–133.

Holland, D., Lachicotte, W., Skinner, D., & Cain, C. (1998). *Identity and agency in cultural worlds.* Cambridge, MA: Harvard University Press.

Holmes, S.L., Land, L.D., & Hinton-Hudson, V.D. (2007). Race still matters: Considerations for mentoring Black women in academe. *Negro Educational Review, 58*(1/2), 105–129.

Hondagneu-Sotelo, P. (1992). Overcoming patriarchal constraints: The reconstruction of gender relations among Mexican immigrant women and women. *Gender and Society, 6*, 393–415.

hooks, b. (1981). *Ain't I a woman? Black women and feminism.* Cambridge, MA: South End Press.

———. (1989). *Talking back: Thinking feminist, thinking Black.* Boston: South End Press.

———. (1993). *Sisters of the yam: Black women and recovery.* Cambridge, MA: South End Press.

———. (1994). *Teaching to transgress.* New York: Routledge.

———. (2000). *All about love: New visions.* New York: William Morrow.

Hope, L.L. (2005). *The Bobbsey twins.* Rockville, MD: Wildside Press.

Hudson-Weems, C. (1993). *Africana womanism: Reclaiming ourselves.* Troy, MI: Bedford Publishers.

———. (1998). Africana womanism. In O. Nnaemeka (Ed.), *Sisterhood: Feminisms and power—from Africa to the Diaspora.* Trenton, NJ: Africa World Press.

Hull, A.G. (2001). *Soul talk: The new spirituality of African American women.* Rochester, VT: Inner Traditions.

Irvine, F., Roberts, G., & Bradbury-Jones, C. (2008). The researcher as insider versus the researcher as outsider: Enhancing rigour through language and cultural sensitivity. *Social Indicators Research Series, 34*, 35–48.

Jekielek, S., Moore, K., & Hair, E. (2002). *Mentoring programs and youth development: A synthesis.* Washington, DC: Child Trends, Inc. ERIC ED 465457.

Johnson, C., Smith, P., & the WGBH Series Research Team. (1998). *Africans in America: America's journey through slavery*. New York: Harcourt.

Kamya, H. (1997). African immigrants in the United States: The challenge for research and practice. *Social Work, 42*(2), 154–165.

Kasinitz, P. (1992). *Caribbean New York: Black immigrants and the politics of race*. Ithaca, NY: Cornell University Press.

Keating, A., & Gonzalez-Lopez, G. (Eds.). (2011). *Bridging: How Gloria Anzaldúa's life and work transformed our own*. Austin: University of Texas Press.

King, J.E. (2005). *Black education: A transformative research and action agenda for the new century*. Washington, DC, & Mahwah, NJ: AERA and Lawrence Erlbaum.

Kohli, R., & Solorzano, D.G. (2012). Teachers, please learn our names! Racial microaggressions and the K–12 classroom. *Race Ethnicity and Education, 15*(4), 441–462.

Kusow, A. (2006). Migration and racial formations among Somali immigrations in North America. *Journal of Ethnic and Migration Studies, 32*(3), 533–551.

Ladner, J. (1981). Tanzanian women and nation building. In F.C. Steady (Ed.), *The Black woman cross-culturally* (pp. 107–117). Rochester, VT: Schenkman Books.

Ladson-Billings, G. (2001). *Crossing over to Canaan: The journey of new teachers in diverse classrooms*. San Francisco, CA: Jossey-Bass.

Landale, N.S., Thomas, K.J.A., & Van Hook, J. (2011). The living arrangements of children of immigrants. *Future of Children, 21*(1), 43–70.

Larose, S., Cyrenne, D., Garceau, O., Harvey, M., Guay, F., Gochin, F., et al. (2011). Academic mentoring and dropout prevention for students in math, science and technology. *Mentoring and Tutoring: Partnership in Learning, 19*(4), 419–439.

Lee, R.M. (2005). Resilience against discrimination: Ethnic identity and other-group orientation as protective factors for Korean Americans. *Journal of Counseling Psychology*, 52(1), 36–44.

Legg, S. (2004). Memory and nostalgia. *Cultural Geographies, 11*, 99–107.

Lieberson, S. (2000). *A matter of taste: How names, fashions, and culture change*. New Haven, CT : Yale University Press.

Lorde, A. (1984). *Sister outsider*. Freedom, CA: The Crossing Press.

Marshall, P. (1983). *Praisesong for the widow*. New York: Penguin.

Mazrui, A. (2000). Cultural amnesia, cultural nostalgia and false memory: Africa's identity crisis revisited. *African Philosophy, 13*(2), 87–98.

Mbilinyi, M. (1984). Research priorities in women's studies in Eastern Africa. *Women's Studies International Forum, 7*(4), 289–300.

McEwen, M.K., Roper, L.D., Bryant, D.R., & Langa, M.J. (1990). Incorporating the development of African-American students into psychosocial theories of development. *Journal of College Student Development, 31*(5), 429–436.

Moghadam, V. (2008). Feminism, legal reform and women's empowerment in the Middle East and North Africa. *International Social Science Journal, 59*(191), 9–16.

Moraga, C., & Anzaldúa, G. (1981). *This bridge called my back: Writings by radical women of color*. Watertown, MA: Persephone Press.

National Archives website (http://www.archives.org).

Nnaemeka, O. (Ed.). (1998). *Sisterhood: Feminisms and power—From Africa to the Diaspora*. Trenton, NJ: Africa World Press.

Noddings, N. (1999). Care, justice, and equity. In M.S. Katz, N. Noddings, & K.A. Strike (Eds.), *Justice and caring: The search for common ground in education* (pp. 7–19). New York: Teachers College Press.

———. (2002). *Educating moral people*. New York: Teachers College Press.

Ofovwe, C.E., & Awaritefe, A. (2009). An exploratory study of the meaning and perception of names among students in a Nigerian university. *African Journal for the Psychological Study of Social Issues, 12*(1/2), 560–581.

Ogbu, J.U. (1987). Variability in minority school performance: A problem in search of an explanation. *Anthropology and Education Quarterly, 18*, 313–334.

Ogundipe-Leslie, O. (1994). *Re-creating ourselves: African women and critical transformations*. Trenton, NJ: Africa World Press.

Okpalaoka, C.L. (2009a). *"You don't look like one, so how are you African?" How West African immigrant girls in the U.S. learn to re-negotiate ethnic identities in home and school contexts*. Unpublished doctoral dissertation, Ohio State University, Columbus, Ohio.

———. (2009b). *On naming: Colonialism and connectedness in Black women's experience*. Unpublished manuscript, Ohio State University, Columbus, OH.

Okpalaoka, C.L., & Dillard, C.B. (2011). Our healing is next to the wound: Endarkened feminisms, spirituality and the wisdom of Sisters of the Yam. In E. J. Tisdale & A. Swartz (Eds.), Adult education and the pursuit of wisdom, *New Directions for Adult and Continuing Education*, 131, 65–73.

———. (2012). (Im)migrations, relations, and identities of African peoples: Toward an endarkened transnational feminist praxis in education. *Educational Foundations, 26*(1/2), 121–142.

Olson, L. (2000). Children of change. 2000 & beyond: The changing face of American students. *Education Week, 20*(4), 1–3. Retrieved from http://www.eric.ed.gov.proxy.lib.ohiostate.edu/PDFS/ED458326.pdf

Omi, M., & Winant, H. (1986). *Racial formation in the United States: From the 1960s to the 1980s.* New York: Routledge & Kegan Paul.

Onimode, B. (1982). *Imperialism and underdevelopment in Nigeria: The dialectics of mass poverty.* London: Zed Press.

Osbon, D.K. (1991). *Reflections on the art of living: A Joseph Campbell companion.* New York: HarperCollins.

Oyewumi, O. (1997). *The invention of women: Making an African sense of Western gender discourses.* Minneapolis: University of Minnesota Press.

Parrillo, V. (1997). *Strangers to these shores: Race and ethnic relations in the United States.* Boston: Allyn & Bacon.

Patton, L. (2009). My sister's keeper: A qualitative examination of mentoring experiences among African American women in graduate and professional schools. *Journal of Higher Education, 80*(5), 510–537.

Petersen, R. (1995). Colonialism as seen from a former colonized area. *Arctic Anthropolgy, 32*(2), 118–126.

Phinney, J. (1989). Stages of ethnic identity in minority group adolescents. *Journal of Early Adolescence, 9*, 34–49.

Phinney, J., & Alipuria, L. (1990). Ethnic identity in college students from four ethnic groups. *Journal of Adolescence, 13*, 171–184.

Pinto, S. (2010). "Why must all girls want to be flag women?" Postcolonial sexualities, national reception, and Caribbean Soca performance. *Meridians: Feminism, Race, Transnationalism, 10*(1), 137–163.

Portes, A., & Rumbaut, R. (2001). *Legacies: the story of the immigrant second generation.* New York: Russell Sage Foundation.

Pryce, J., Silverton, N., & Sanchez, B. (2010). GirlPOWER! Strengthening mentoring relationships through a structured, gender-specific program. *New Directions for Youth Development, 126*, 89–105.

Quarles, A., Maldonado, N., & Lacey, C. (2005, March). *Mentoring at-risk adolescent girls: A phenomenological investigation.* Paper presented at the Annual meeting of the American Educational Research Association, Montreal, Canada.

Quintana, S.M., Castaneda-English, P., & Ybarra, V.C. (1999). Role of perspective-taking abilities and ethnic socialization in development of adolescent ethnic identity. *Journal of Research on Adolescence, 9*(2), 161–184.

Reid, I. (1938). Negro immigration to the United States. *Social Forces, 16*(3), 411–417.

Reismann, F. (1962). *The culturally deprived child.* New York: Harper & Row.

Rockefeller Foundation, New York. *The Rockefeller Foundation 1964 Annual Report.* http://www.rockefellerfoundation.org/uploads/files/3c97a37d-7c73-4db4-b395-7168edf9d0ed-1964.pdf

Rodriguez, J., & Fortier, T. (2007). *Cultural memory: Resistance, faith, and identity.* Austin: University of Texas Press.

Rong, X., & Brown, F. (2001). The effects of immigrant generation and ethnicity on educational attainment among young African and Caribbean Blacks in the United States. *Harvard Educational Review, 71*(3), 536–565.

———. (2002a). Socialization, culture, and identities of Black immigrant children: What educators need to know. *Education and Urban Society, 34*(2), 247–273.

———. (2002b). Immigration and urban education in the new millennium: The diversity and the challenges. *Education and Urban Society, 34*(2), 123–133.

Rong, X., & Preissle, J. (1998). *Educating immigrant students: What educators need to know to meet the challenges.* Thousand Oaks, CA: Corwin Press.

Rosenthal, D. A., & Feldman, S.S. (1992). The relationship between parenting behavior and ethnic identity in Chinese-American and Chinese-Australian adolescents. *International Journal of Psychology, 27*(1), 19–31.

Rothbard, S. (2005). Your name is your name. *Paterson Literary Review, 34,* 317.

Russell, M. (1982). Black-eyed blues connections: Teaching Black women. In G.T. Hull, P.B. Scott, & B. Smith (Eds.), *All the women are white, all the Blacks are men, but some of us are brave* (pp. 196–207). NY: The Feminist Press.

Ryan, E. B., Carranza, M. A., & Moffie, R. W. (1977). Reactions toward varying degrees of accentedness in the speech of Spanish-English bilinguals. *Language and Speech, 20,* 267–273.

Ryan, J.S. (2005). *Spirituality as ideology in Black women's film and literature.* Charlottesville: University of Virginia Press.

Sabatier, C. (2008). Ethnic and national identity among second-generation immigrant adolescents in France: The role of social context and family. *Journal of Adolescence, 31,* 185–205.

Sandoval, S.R., Gutkin, T.B., & Naumann, W.C. (1997). Racial identity attitudes and school performance among African American high school students: An exploratory study. *Research in Schools, 4,* 1–8.

Savin-Williams, R., & Berndt, T.J. (1990). Friendship and peer relations. In S. Feldman & G. Elliot (Eds.), *At the threshold* (pp. 277–307). Cambridge, MA: Harvard University Press.

Seaton, E., Scottham, K., & Sellers, R. (2006). The status model of racial identity development in African American adolescents: Evidence of structure, trajectories, and well-being. *Child Development, 77*(5), 1416–1426.

Shadiow, L.K. (2009). The first day of class: How it matters. *Clearing House: A Journal of Educational Strategies, Issues and Ideas, 82*(4), 197–200.

Smith, D. (1979). A sociology for women. In J. Sherman & E. Beck (Eds.), *The prism of sex: Essays in the sociology of knowledge*. Madison: University of Wisconsin Press.

Soyinka-Airewele, P. (2005). Postcolonial angst and the Nigerian scholarly estate. *Journal of Third World Studies, 32*(1), 109–133.

Steady, F.C. (1981). The Black woman cross-culturally: An overview. In F.C. Steady (Ed.), *The Black woman cross-culturally*. Cambridge, MA: Schenkman Publishing.

Steady, F.C. (1996). African feminism: A worldwide perspective. In R. Terbog-Penn & R. Benton (Eds.), *Women in Africa: A reader* (2nd ed.) Washington, DC: Howard University Press.

———. (2004). An investigative framework for gender research in Africa in the new millennium. In *CODESRIA, African gender scholarship: Concepts, methodologies and paradigms* (pp. 42–60). Dakar, Senegal: CODESRIA.

Stewart, D. (1993). *Immigration and education: The crisis and the opportunities*. New York: Lexington Books.

Stritikus, T., & Nguyen, D. (2007). Strategic transformation: Gender identity negotiation in first generation Vietnamese youth. *American Educational Research Journal,* 44 (4), 853–895.

Student cries foul when professor mispronounces his name. (2008, January). *Dean & Provost,* 9(5), 10-10.

Suárez-Orozco, C. (1999). *Conceptual considerations in our understanding of immigrant adolescent girls*. Paper presented at the Annual Convention of the American Psychological Association, Boston, MA, August 20–24, 1999.

Suárez-Orozco, C., & Suárez-Orozco, M. (1995). *Transformations: Migration, family life, and achievement motivation among Latino adolescents*. Stanford, CA: Stanford University Press.

Suárez-Orozco, C., & Todorova, I. (2003). Understanding the social world of immigrant youth. In C. Suárez-Orozco & I. Todorova (Eds.), *New Directions for Youth Development: Theory, Practice, and Research, 100*. San Francisco, CA: Jossey-Bass.

Sue, C.A., & Telles, E.E. (2007). Assimilation and gender in naming. *American Journal of Sociology, 112,* 1383–1415.

Super, C., & Harkness, S. (1997). The cultural structuring of child development. In J. Berry, P. Dasen, and T. Saraswathi (Eds.). *Handbook of Cross-Cultural Psychology: Vol. 2. Basic Processes and Human Development* (2nd ed.). (pp.1–39). Boston: Allyn and Bacon.

Takaki, R. (1998). *Strangers from a different shore: A history of Asian Americans* (rev. ed.). Boston: Little, Brown.

Takougang, J. (1995). Recent African immigrants to the United States: A historical perspective. *Western Journal of Black Studies, 19*(1), 50–57.

Takougang, J., & Tidjani, B. (2009). Settlement patterns and organizations among African immigrants in the United States. *Journal of Third World Studies, 26*(1), 31–40.

Tatum, B.D. (1997). *Why are all the Black kids sitting together in the cafeteria? And other conversations about race.* New York: Basic Books.

Trans Atlantic Slave Trade African Names database (http://slavevoyages.org).

Traore, R. (2003). African students in America: Reconstructing new meanings of African American in urban education. *Intercultural Education, 14*(3), 243–254.

———. (2006). Voices of African students in America: "We're not from the jungle." *Multicultural Perspectives, 8*(2), 29–34.

Traore, R., & Lukens, R. (2006). *"This isn't the America I thought I'd find": African students in the urban U.S. high school.* Lanham, MD: University Press of America.

Travis, R. (2010). What they think: Attributions made by youth workers about youth circumstances and the implications for service-delivery in out-of-school programs. *Child Youth Care Forum, 39*, 443–464.

Trueba, H.T. (1999). *Latinos Unidos: From cultural diversity to the politics of solidarity.* New York: Rowman & Littlefield.

Trueba, H.T., & Bartolome, L. (Eds.). (2000). *Immigrant voices: In search of educational equity.* New York: Rowman & Littlefield.

Tsolidis, G. (2011). Memories of home: Family in the Diaspora. *Journal of Comparative Family Studies, 42*(3), 411–420.

Tuhiwai-Smith, L. (1999). *Decolonizing methodologies: Research and indigenous peoples.* London: Zed Books.

Umana-Taylor, A.J. & Fine, M.A. (2004). Examining a model of ethnic identity development among Mexican-origin adolescents living in the U.S. *Hispanic Journal of Behavioral Sciences, 26*, 36–59.

Umana-Taylor, A.J., Bhanot, R., & Shin, N. (2006). Ethnic identity formation during adolescence: The critical role of families. *Journal of Family Issues, 27*(3), 390–414.

U.S. Department of Education, Office of Educational Research and Improvement, National Institute for the Education of At-Risk Students. (1998). *Facts about limited English proficient students.* Washington, DC: Author.

Vaquera, E., & Kao, G. (2006). The implications of choosing "no race" on the salience of Hispanic identity: How racial and ethnic backgrounds intersect among Hispanic adolescents. *Sociological Quarterly*, 47(3), 375–396.

Wade-Gayles, G. (Ed.). (1995). *My soul is a witness: African American women's spirituality*. Boston: Beacon Press.

Wakefield, W.D., & Hudley, C. (2007). Ethnic and racial identity and adolescent well-being. *Theory into Practice*, 46(2), 147–154.

Walker, A. (1983). *In search of our mothers' gardens*. New York: Harcourt.

———. (2006). *We are the ones we have been waiting for: Inner light in a time of darkness*. New York: The New Press.

Waters, M. (1989). The everyday use of surname to determine ethnic ancestry. *Qualitative Sociology*, 12(3), 303–324.

———. (1991). The role of lineage in identity formation among Black Americans. *Qualitative Sociology*, 14, 57–76.

———. (1994). Ethnic and racial identities of second-generation Black immigrants in New York City. *International Migration Review*, 28, 795–820.

Watkins., S. C. & London, A.S. (1994). Personal names and cultural change: A study of the naming patterns of Italians and Jews in the United States in 1910. *Social Science History*, 18(2), 169–209.

Watson, M. (2005). Africans to America: The unfolding of identity. *Irinkerindo: A Journal of African Migration*, 4, 1–11.

Western Kentucky University website. http://people.wku.edu/johnston.njoku/freedomtrailwhole.html.

What's in a name? Perhaps a student's grade. (2005). *American School Board Journal*, 192(8).

Wilkerson, I. (2010). *The warmth of other suns: The epic story of America's great migration*. New York: Random House.

William, I. (2009). Post-colonialism, memory and the remaking of African identity. *Politikon*, 36(3), 423–443.

Wilson, S. (1998). *The means of naming: A social and cultural history of personal naming in Western Europe*. London: UCL Press.

Yewah, E. (2008). Undoing and reconstructing African identities: A cultural approach. *African Identities*, 6(1), 17–28.

Young, A.L. (1999). Archaeological investigations of slave housing at Saragossa Plantation, Natchez, Mississippi. *Southeastern Archaeology*, 18(1).

Zhou, M. (1999). Coming of age: The current situation of Asian American children. *Amerasia Journal*, 25(1), 1–27.

ROCHELLE BROCK &
RICHARD GREGGORY JOHNSON III,
Executive Editors

Black Studies and Critical Thinking is an interdisciplinary series which examines the intellectual traditions of and cultural contributions made by people of African descent throughout the world. Whether it is in literature, art, music, science, or academics, these contributions are vast and far-reaching. As we work to stretch the boundaries of knowledge and understanding of issues critical to the Black experience, this series offers a unique opportunity to study the social, economic, and political forces that have shaped the historic experience of Black America, and that continue to determine our future. Black Studies and Critical Thinking is positioned at the forefront of research on the Black experience, and is the source for dynamic, innovative, and creative exploration of the most vital issues facing African Americans. The series invites contributions from all disciplines but is specially suited for cultural studies, anthropology, history, sociology, literature, art, and music.

Subjects of interest include (but are not limited to):

- EDUCATION
- SOCIOLOGY
- HISTORY
- MEDIA/COMMUNICATION
- RELIGION/THEOLOGY
- WOMEN'S STUDIES

- POLICY STUDIES
- ADVERTISING
- AFRICAN AMERICAN STUDIES
- POLITICAL SCIENCE
- LGBT STUDIES

For additional information about this series or for the submission of manuscripts, please contact Dr. Brock (Indiana University Northwest) at brock2@iun.edu or Dr. Johnson (University of San Francisco) at rgjohnsoniii@usfca.edu.

To order other books in this series, please contact our Customer Service Department:

(800) 770-LANG (within the U.S.)
(212) 647-7706 (outside the U.S.)
(212) 647-7707 FAX

Or browse online by series at www.peterlang.com.

www.ingramcontent.com/pod-product-compliance
Ingram Content Group UK Ltd.
Pitfield, Milton Keynes, MK11 3LW, UK
UKHW021849210426
5322IPUK00022B/560